VOLUME 44

NORTHROP
F-5/F-20/T-38

FREDERICK A. JOHNSEN

specialtypress

PUBLISHERS AND WHOLESALERS

Published by
Specialty Press Publishers and Wholesalers
39966 Grand Avenue
North Branch, MN 55056
United States of America
(800) 895-4585 or (651) 277-1400
www.specialtypress.com

COPYRIGHT © 2006 BY FREDERICK A. JOHNSEN

ISBN-13 978-1-58007-214-4
Item # SP094P

Cover: Brazilian F-5E was photographed with enlarged dorsal fin visible. (Northrop via Craig Kaston collection)

Title Page: The first and third Freedom Fighters settled in to land at Williams Air Force Base, Arizona. Both leading and trailing edge flaps are deployed. (Air Force via Challen "Choni" Irvine collection)

Back Cover:
Top: Carrying an air-to-surface missile shape on the centerline, F-20 N4416T employed a two-tone gray camouflage scheme at the time of this photograph. The small F-20 test and demonstration fleet underwent several paint changes. (AFFTC/HO collection)

Middle: All the glamour of high-speed jet fighter flight test programs comes to life in a brilliant color photo of the first N-156F (59-4987) banking over Edwards Air Force Base, its ventral speed brakes deployed. Years later, this same Freedom Fighter prototype, again painted silver and orange, would be displayed in the Museum of Flight in Seattle, Washington. (Northrop via Craig Kaston collection)

Bottom: Head-on view of a T-38A shows stand-off inlets far enough from the fuselage surface to avoid boundary layer air turbulence. "Coke bottle" area-rule phenomenon is clearly visible in narrowing of fuselage at wing junction. (AFFTC/HO collection)

TABLE OF CONTENTS

PREFACE

A few well-placed strokes of India ink rendered this flight view of the first N-156F. (Northrop via Craig Kaston collection)

Its curvy good looks set the diminutive F-5 ahead of the pack. In an era when some Cold War allies of the United States still flew cast-off World War II propeller-driven bombers and fighters, in the late 1950s Northrop seized on the need to deliver modern warplanes with modest maintenance requirements, to enable the shapers of American foreign policy to economically give allies supersonic performance. If the U.S. Air Force and Navy only tangentially used the F-5, decades of new American fliers honed their skills on the similar T-38 variant.

The compilation of this account was boosted by many people (some now deceased) from many disciplines, spanning decades. Thanks especially to the Abbotsford International Air Show Society (and Ron Thornber), Air Force Flight Test Center History Office (and Jeannine Geiger and Freida Johnson), Peter M. Bowers, Canadian Air Force, Experimental Aircraft Association (EAA), Flight Test Historical Museum (and Doug and Ilah Nelson), Dennis Jenkins, Kenneth G. Johnsen, John Lisella, LCDR Chad Mingo, Pacific Northwest Aviation Historical Foundation (and Harl V. Brackin, Jr.), Bill Rippy, Barrett Tillman, and Terry Vanden-Heuvel (AMARC Public Affairs).

And my wife Sharon proved to be more than a good sport about the demands of this project. The Skoshi Tiger chapter is possible only because of her tireless copying of hundreds of pages of source documents at the Air Force Historical Research Agency (AFHRA) during a whirlwind research visit. AFHRA's affable Archie Difante and the agency staff once again proved to be crucial to the success of that visit.

Some of the people who helped deserve a bit more than just the appearance of their name here. Specifically, it has been a big help to have Northrop professionals like Bill Flanagan, Tony Chong, Craig Kaston, and Ron Gibb run their eyes over this manuscript. Their enthusiastic sharing of F-5 knowledge is reassuring. Tony and Craig bring the additional credentials of being world-class photo collectors. Ron Gibb has an amazing 40 years of F-5 engineering experience to his credit. Bill Flanagan is a remarkable Renaissance man of aviation.

While completing this manuscript, it was my very good fortune to have a long lunch with retired Air Force Gen. Bob Titus, who commanded the 10th Fighter Commando Squadron, flying F-5Cs, in Vietnam, and Challen W. Irvine (Martini), who flew with General Titus. I came away impressed with the irrepressible fighter-pilot independence, nonetheless wrapped in graciousness, exhibited by these two tigers—Skoshi Tigers.

Diligent volunteers with the Dutch Aviation Society/Scramble have compiled an extensive web site characterizing many of the world's air forces, including users of F-5s, which proved most interesting and helpful.

The pleasure of researching historical events is enhanced by reviewing literature contemporary with the topic under discussion. For the F-5 story, the authoritative, concise, workmanlike reportage in professional trade publications like Aviation Week & Space Technology magazine dating back to the late 1950s is neatly surrounded by advertisements touting Cold War necessities, and stories of political realities that sometimes seem archaic, and other times remain startlingly germane. The F-5 did not incubate in a vacuum. It was a product of onrushing technological breakthroughs that shaped, and were shaped by, world events. The global acceptance of the F-5, and the remarkable longevity of the T-38, stand in tribute to the vision that created this cost-effective series of sleek speedsters.

Readers familiar with the WarbirdTech series know that a key feature of these volumes is technical art and information from official manuals and sources. In this F-5 story, official reports are sometimes quoted directly at length, to further enhance the reader's sense of seeing the same information decision-makers had access to during the development of this remarkable series of aircraft. Poring over reams of documentation, it has become evident that even official sources disagree on some points. Effort has been made to keep statistical data as accurate as possible in this volume, but some variation occasionally occurs. Nonetheless, what emerges is a chronicle of an outstanding, forward-looking series of supersonic jet aircraft from Northrop that first took wing in the late 1950s. Some members of that family tree still serve as this is being written. It has been a fast, and long, ride through history.

—Frederick A. Johnsen
December 2005

THE F-5 FREEDOM FIGHTER

With the sleek F-5 series, Northrop executed an aesthetic blend of simplicity and capability that ultimately garnered customers from around the world. The F-5 bucked military aircraft design rationale when it was conceived in the mid-1950s, but that is not surprising—it came from Northrop, a company known for innovation. As early as 1954, Northrop's deputy chief engineer (and later Northrop chairman), Tom Jones, espoused the concept of "life cost" to explain and define the true value of an aircraft. Jones reasoned the actual cost of an airplane is not its initial purchase price, but the cost of using it throughout its service life.

This notion was particularly important for countries with defense budgets smaller than those committed annually by the United States and the Soviet Union. In the heady urgency of the Cold War arms race, many American designs strove for highest performance, regardless of cost, during the life of the system. This could lead to super aircraft that were too expensive for less wealthy allies to buy or maintain. It was the era of the Century Series of jet fighters, beginning with the F-100. A gulf was widening between the capabilities of the front-line fighters of America and the aging second- and third-string warplanes of U.S. allies.

The Northrop philosophy of simple, lightweight fighters was brought to bear on a company study designated N-102, and called "Fang." The brainchild of Northrop's chief of preliminary

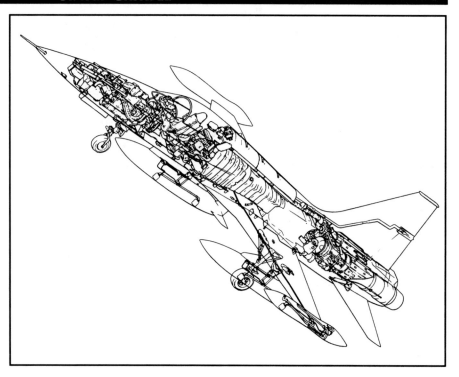

Early Northrop drawings depicted F-5A and B-model airframe structure. B-models did not carry 20-mm cannons. (Northrop via AFFTC/HO collection)

Early silver F-5As each lugged a 1,000-lb centerline-mounted bomb plus fuel tanks and smaller ordnance. F-5A coating of silver paint generally gave way to camouflage schemes desired by customers. (Challen Irvine collection)

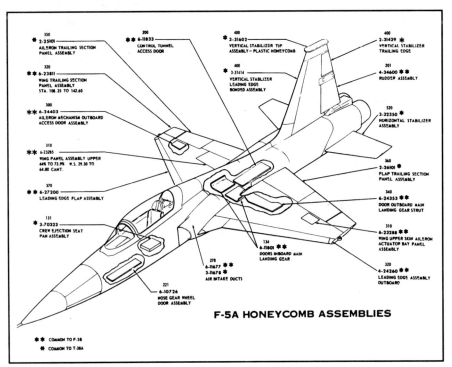

F-5A HONEYCOMB ASSEMBLIES

** COMMON TO F-5B
* COMMON TO T-38A

The F-5 pioneered extensive use of honeycomb structure, as detailed in Northrop drawings of A- and B-model Freedom Fighters. (AFFTC/HO collection)

design, Welko Gasich, and Edgar Schmued, Northrop vice president engineering, the N-102 never went beyond a mock-up that depicted a diminutive high-wing, single-tail, single-engine speedster. The N-102 concept promoted a host of swap-out options including changing the kind of guns and even the model of jet engine in the field; the later F-5 project would be more modest in this area. Fang was said to be ini-

tially more expensive per pound of airframe than traditional designs, but in keeping with Northrop's life cost philosophy, the company forecast a lower cost throughout the N-102's life because of its designed-in convertibility. A Fang tenet that surfaced in the F-5 program was easy access for servicing via hinged or removable panels.[1] Subsequently the F-5's progenitors, the N-156Fs, had more than 25 percent of the fuselage area made up of doors or removable panels. In Northrop genealogy, the unbuilt N-102 is a conceptual milepost that fostered subsequent F-5 creation.

Embracing life cost tenets, Northrop designers sought a way to create a competitive jet fighter that was affordable for America's allies. The new fighter would be lightweight, low in initial price as well as ongoing costs, and powered by engines that produced a high thrust-to-weight ratio. The notion of high thrust-to-weight was another concept not universally appreciated in the 1950s. It could keep Northrop's new fighter nimble enough to hold its own even in combats with faster Mach 2 fighters.

As Northrop continued to evolve its fighter premise, General Electric was busy perfecting the relatively small SJ-110 turbojet engine that would become the reliable J85 high thrust-to-weight powerplant of the F-5 and the T-38. Evolved from a turbojet conceived for missile applications, two of the efficient J85s could be nested side by side in the F-5. Another contender briefly mentioned for the T-38 engine in 1957–1958 was Fairchild's competing high thrust-to-weight J83.

Northrop's rationale for using two J85s can be visualized by comparing other jet engines of the period, as seen in the following table:

Jet Engine Thrust-to-Weight Ratio Data[2]			
	Weight (lbs)	Max Thrust (lbs)	Thrust/Wt. Ratio
J47 w/afterburner	3,200	7,650	2.4
J79-7 w/afterburner	3,375	15,800	4.7
Two J85-13s w/afterburners	1,195	8,160	6.8

As Northrop was refining the small airframe, it took advantage of the small, yet powerful, J85s. Discussions with General Electric led to redesigning parts of the J85 to relocate some engine-mounted accessories beneath the engines instead of atop them, to better accommodate available space in the F-5 fuselage.[3]

Northrop's first iteration of this lightweight fighter, bearing company designation N-156, was a 1955 T-tail speedster weighing less than 10,000 lbs. It was pitched to the U.S. Navy as an ideal jet for use on small so-called jeep carriers. A subsequent decision to take the jeep carriers out of service ended this developmental avenue for Northrop before an aircraft was built. Mean-

while, the N-156 design matured with features including an area-rule fuselage design to facilitate acceleration from subsonic to supersonic speeds. This gave the F-5 its characteristic slim-waisted appearance.

When the U.S. Air Force sought a new supersonic trainer in the mid-1950s to replace the older subsonic T-33, Northrop further evolved its N-156 design to create what became the successful and long-lived T-38 Talon. The Air Force issued, in May 1955, its general operation requirement (GOR) for a trainer referred to as TZ. Variously

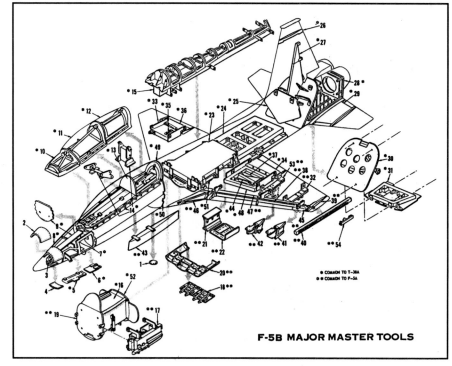

To make the F-5 required master tooling, as depicted in a Northrop drawing for the F-5B. Items with single asterisks beside their number were common also to the T-38A; items with double asterisks were common to the F-5A. (AFFTC/HO collection)

F-5B MAJOR MASTER TOOLS

The second F-5B (63-8439) in take-off view shows scalloped F-5 engine inlet that is a quick recognition tool to differentiate two-seat F-5Bs from similar T-38s, as is the presence of area-rule tip tanks on F-5Bs. (USAF via Challen Irvine)

identified as N-156T in company nomenclature, and then TZ-156, the Talon ultimately received military trainer designation T-38. A full-scale mock-up of the TZ-156 in 1956 bore a strong resemblance to the final T-38 design, although the TZ-156 initially showed a swept vertical tail instead of the characteristic trapezoid vertical fin and rudder actually used on T-38s and F-5s. Capitalizing on the priority placed by the Air Force on getting its own supersonic trainer built, Northrop flew the first T-38 on 10 April 1959.[4]

Even as the T-38 was taking form, its success encouraged Northrop's design team to continue pushing for a lightweight fighter variant that could be furnished to America's allies. Company funds were used to begin constructing a prototype N-156F fighter in early 1958. That May, a letter of intent from the U.S. government authorized Northrop to build not one, but three, N-156F prototype export fighters.

The first N-156F, assigned Air Force serial 59-4987, rolled out of the Northrop plant on the last day of May 1959. Shipped to the Air Force Flight Test Center at Edwards Air Force Base in California's Mojave Desert, 987 first flew 30 July 1959, with Northrop's Lew Nelson in the cockpit. Engines for the first N-156F initially were non-after-burning General Electric J85-GE-1 models; even with this limitation, the N-156F went supersonic on its first flight. Aircraft 59-4987 and 59-4988 were finished and flown as N-156Fs. The third N-156F's completion was halted, and it ultimately emerged as a YF-5A, still bearing serial 59-4989.

Shared Pedigree

The Northrop design team managed to keep the F-5 and its T-38 trainer sibling economically viable in part by using shared structures where feasible. Basic wing planform of the T-38, with a 32-degree leading edge sweepback, was retained and modified with leading edge devices for the F-5. This wing delivered handling qualities desirable for a trainer by minimizing pitch-up due to wingtip stall. This was accomplished by using the relatively modest sweepback. Overall the wing design was a reasonable compromise of supersonic drag traits and handling qualities.

The final design configuration of the T-38 stood as the baseline for creating the F-5.[5]

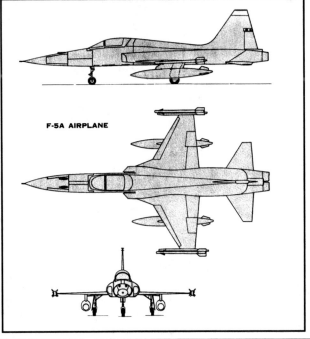

Northrop F-5A three-view drawing shows wing leading edge extensions fairing into inlets. A-model extensions were much smaller than those ultimately developed for the F-5E and F-20 models. (AFFTC/HO collection)

F-5A AIRPLANE

Northrop's testbed F-5A in the summer of 1965 used a two-position nosewheel strut to facilitate shorter takeoff rolls. (Northrop via Craig Kaston collection)

Left: In the summer of 1965 Northrop used an F-5A (63-8421) to test upgrades including auxiliary air doors on the sides of the fuselage just ahead of the J85 engines. The doors improved engine performance in the low-speed range during takeoff and landing. (Northrop via Tony Chong collection)

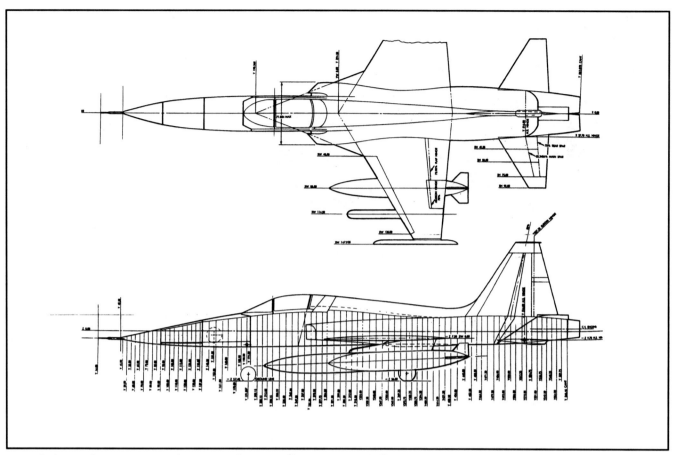

Detailed Northrop stations drawings show similarities and differences between F-5A and F-5B configurations. (AFFTC/HO collection)

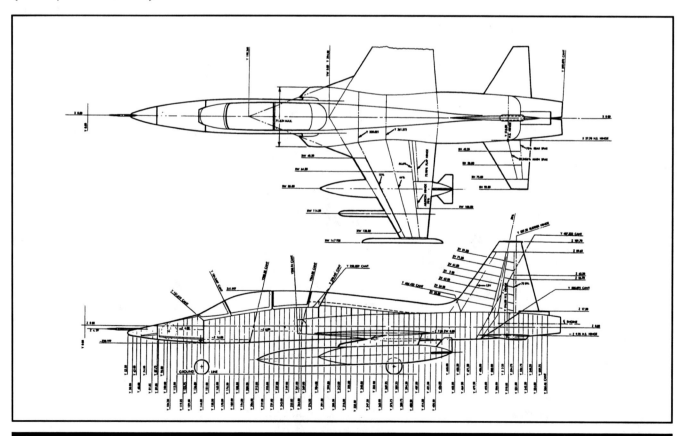

An evolved N-156 mock-up showed the fighter carrying large-finned missile dummies on each wingtip. Inlet design was not finalized when this mock-up was made. (Northrop via Craig Kaston collection)

The original N-156F Freedom Fighter was displayed at an Edwards Air Force Base open house in 1962 with various ordnance hung from hard points. The number one Freedom Fighter later joined the museum collection of the Pacific Northwest Aviation Historical Foundation (PNAHF) in Seattle in 1968, due at least in part to its diminutive size, which enabled the N-156F to fit in the museum's facility near the Space Needle. PNAHF is the founding organization that gave rise to the Museum of Flight on Boeing Field in Seattle. (Peter M. Bowers collection)

Photographed 27 November 1963, the first Freedom Fighter tested area-rule tip tanks with outboard fins that were not adopted for production. (AFFTC/HO collection)

F-5A Described

Northrop described the F-5A in a tooling document as "a supersonic, high performance, jet fighter developed for the Department of Defense to provide flexible, versatile air power for any potential combat environment."[6] The forward fuselage contains avionics, nose landing gear, and a pair of 20-mm cannons. The cannons necessitated ducting for removal of gunfire gases, plus chutes for "ammunition, case ejection, and clip transfer," according to the tooling description.

An alternate F-5A nose holds cameras for reconnaissance. (The resulting RF-5A reconnaissance jet did not typically interchange the recon nose with the fighter nose, although some variants like Canadian Freedom Fighters did have the ability to switch.) The forward fuselage also contains the cockpit, enclosed by a wraparound windscreen and a rearward-hinging canopy. Construction of the fuselage is a semi-monocoque aluminum structure. According to the tooling book, "Almost all the frames and skins in this section are chem-milled to some degree in order to reduce the overall weight."[7]

The center fuselage includes integral air inlets and ducts, six wing attach fittings, and a machined and canted bulkhead to support the vertical stabilizer main spar and outboard engine mounts. Some center fuselage skins are aluminum; others are magnesium. These skins are also chem-milled. Three fuel cell bladders nest between the intake ducts; a dorsal fairing has removable panels to access two bladder fuel cells.[8]

The semi-monocoque aft fuselage, near the hot engine exhaust, uses stainless steel formers with

titanium inner segments, as well as firewalls made of titanium using ceramic gold coating. Chem-milled magnesium outer skins enclose the aft fuselage. Actuator mechanism and hinge bearings for the horizontal stabilizers are in the lower forward portion of the aft fuselage. The entire aft fuselage is removable for engine access, and is considered an interchangeable component of the F-5A. The seam for this removable section is angled in such a way that ample engine bay access is provided while allowing the vertical fin and rudder to remain attached to the rest of the fuselage instead of coming off as was common with jet fighters of the day. Northrop engineers estimated that this feature saved 100 lbs in structural weight for the F-5/T-38.

To stay within the outer mold line designed for the tapered aft fuselage while still accommodating the need for a vertical fin spar passing between the two engines, the J85s are canted, with their exhausts pointing inward two degrees. When early test flights revealed some adverse interaction between the converging exhaust plumes, the addition of fairing between the engine ejectors corrected this.[9]

The F-5A wing is one assembly, running across the aircraft's centerline. Basic construction is multi-spar aluminum alloy. The torque box section of the wing incorporates machined ribs and spars, as well as machined upper and lower skins. Main landing gear mounts to the underside of the wings, retracting inward to nest in the fuselage. Ailerons, flaps, and leading edge devices are hinged to the wing. Some wing components are made of bonded aluminum honeycomb, including leading edge flap devices, the outboard trailing section, flap and aileron trailing sections, outboard leading edge, the area above the main gear strut wells, aileron access doors, and main gear strut doors.[10]

The cockpit of the first N-156F (59-4987) still carried most of its instruments when presented to the Pacific Northwest Aviation Historical Foundation in Seattle, as photographed in November 1973.

Early N-156 mock-up, circa March 1957, showed a number of ideas later culled from the design, like the aft-swept vertical tail, wing trailing edge body fillets, and a three-piece windscreen. Ideas retained include easy access to service the aircraft. (Northrop via Craig Kaston collection)

Speed brakes, conforming to the contour of the lower center fuselage, are attached via supporting structure to the lower surface of the wing. The speed brakes are of hinged, cast, and machined structure.[11]

The vertical stabilizer is traditional built-up ribs with two main spars and machined main skins forming an airfoil shape. The leading edge is aluminum honeycomb. The tip is Fiberglas reinforced polyester with phenolic honeycomb containing an antenna assembly. Two interchangeable rudder hinge fittings are used. The rudder is an aluminum honeycomb adhesive bonded airfoil structure. A hydraulically operated torque tube enables its movement.[12]

The horizontal stabilizer consists of a left and a right control surface built up of riveted spars and ribs combined with aluminum honeycomb. The forged machined main spars become trunnions inside the aft fuselage.

The F-5A was designed to accommodate varied external stores attached to the wings. Pylons at Wing Station 85.00 can carry weapons or 150-gallon fuel tanks. Pylons at Wing Station 114.50 are intended for armament. Wingtip hard points can carry special area-rule fuel tanks or armaments. A fuselage centerline pylon can carry a fuel tank or armament.[13]

Two General Electric J85-GE-13 turbojets with afterburners power the F-5A, each delivering a static thrust measured at 4,080 lbs. Top speed of the F-5A is listed as 925 miles per hour.[14]

F-5B Described

The two-seat F-5B, according to Northrop documentation, is "a

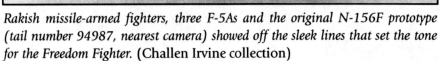

Rakish missile-armed fighters, three F-5As and the original N-156F prototype (tail number 94987, nearest camera) showed off the sleek lines that set the tone for the Freedom Fighter. (Challen Irvine collection)

Bottom view of a Canadian A-model equivalent in flight shows the effects of area rule theory on the fuselage/wing juncture as well as the tip tank/wing intersection.

supersonic high performance twin-jet aircraft developed to provide versatile fighter support of ground forces with the added capability of crew observer surveillance. In addition, the aircraft is capable of providing supersonic flight training..."[15] The forward fuselage placed the pilots in tandem, giving the nose a foreshortened appearance compared with the sleek lines of the single-seat F-5A. The two canopies of the F-5B hinge to swing up and aft.

Northrop very deliberately established a tooling policy to promote "the utilization of common T-38A, F-5A, and F-5B plans, tooling, and production capability to the greatest extent permitted by common or similar design configuration." Northrop described the F-5B as "in most part a combination of

View from beneath and behind a Canadian Air Force CF-5 shows the tip tanks' use of area-rule "wasp waist" design only where the tanks interface with the wingtips, and not on the outboard sides where no area rule demands are made on the shape.

A single-seat Canadian CF-5A leads a pair of CF-5B (or D-for-Dual) Freedom Fighters launching from Paine Field near Everett, Washington, in July 1984. The A-model sports a refueling probe on the right side of the fuselage, instead of on the left as had been done with Skoshi Tiger F-5Cs.

Canadian CF-5D (Dual) lands with its auxiliary engine air doors open on the aft fuselage side just ahead of the base of the vertical fin, July 1983. (Photo by Sharon Lea Johnsen)

Flashing its sculpted belly to the camera, the original N-156F provided a study in area rule and aesthetics. Unlike pinched F-5 tip tanks, rails and air-to-air missiles mounted on the wingtips could not conform to area-rule tenets. (Peter M. Bowers collection)

structural and functional components of the T-38A and the F-5A." [16]

T-38 Described

The supersonic T-38A Talon trainer, though superficially similar in appearance to the F-5B, has some salient differences. A quick recognition feature is the profile of the engine inlets beside the aft cockpit. On T-38As, when viewed from the side, these inlets have an angular lip with the top of the inlet projecting farther forward than the bottom of the inlet in a straight canted line. On F-5Bs, the inlet profile is concave, with the profile curving back from the top of the inlet down to the bottom.

The T-38A was fitted with two General Electric J85-GE-5 turbojet engines with afterburners, each capable, when mounted in the aircraft, of producing 2,050 lbs of thrust in military power and 2,900 lbs of thrust at maximum power (using sea level, standard day calculations). [17] Static thrust calculations for this engine variant (not mounted in the airframe) indicate 3,850 lbs of thrust in afterburner, slightly less than that of the F-5A. Top speed of the T-38A is listed as 820 miles per hour at 36,089 feet. [18]

The T-38's forward fuselage ahead of the cockpits cambers upward to produce forebody lift to counteract downward air load on the nose that otherwise might be brought about by the slopes of the twin canopies.

Minus U.S. insignia, the first N-156F prototype (59-4987) carried Northrop's logo on the tail and the Freedom Fighter name on the nose next to the nomenclature N-156F for a publicity photo early in its career. (Peter M. Bowers collection)

Though seldom seen without either tip tanks or missiles, the N-156F could be flown with a slick wing, as captured in this photo over Edwards Air Force Base ranges. (Peter M. Bowers collection)

The first and third Freedom Fighters settled in to land at Williams Air Force Base, Arizona. Both leading and trailing edge flaps are deployed. (Air Force via Challen "Choni" Irvine collection)

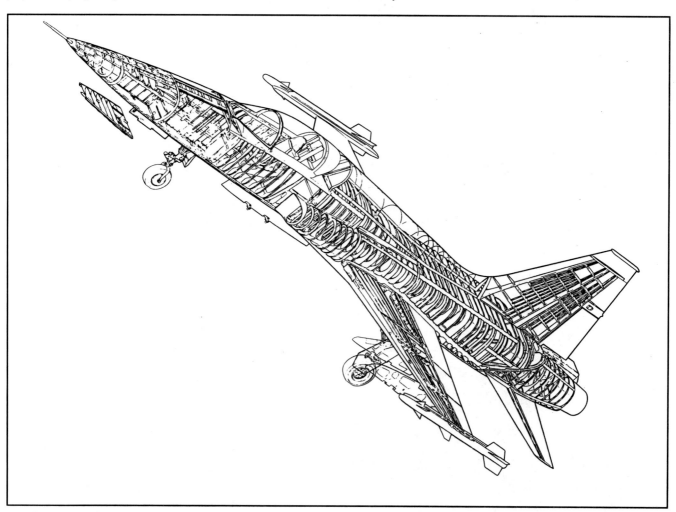

Northrop F-5A skeletal drawing showed location of 20-mm cannons in the nose, as well as fuselage fuel stowage ahead of the engines between the inlet ducts. (AFFTC/HO collection)

The third Freedom Fighter, finished as an F-5A, was photographed from several angles on 15 February 1965 on the hard bed of Rogers Dry Lake at Edwards Air Force Base. Views show an ordnance stores loading including a centerline Mk84, Wing Station 85 Mk 83, Wing Station 115.5 M-117, and wingtip fuel tanks. (AFFTC/HO collection)

The prototype Freedom Fighter tested 50-gallon tip tanks with outboard fins, which were not adopted for production. Some wags said the narrow-waisted tip tanks looked like peanuts, also using the term "peanuts" to refer to the relatively small amount of fuel they could carry. (AFFTC/HO collection)

Getting the Gear Up Faster

The T-38 was so swift that its original main landing-gear retraction system proved insufficient to get the mainwheels retracted before the accelerating jet reached the maximum gear-down speed of 240 knots. Since forcing the aircraft to stay slower than 240 knots while the gear retracted was considered unacceptable because it would mean reducing power after takeoff or establishing a steeper climbout angle, the Northrop team devised a way to help the main gear retract faster. The thin wing precluded installing a larger hydraulic retraction system without bulging its contours. This had an undesirable outcome on aircraft performance—drag.

It was possible to gain some increase in retraction system power by modifying the existing system within the confines of the airframe shape, but the final answer to the retraction speed was the creation of a hinged flap on the trailing edge of the main landing gear strut doors. These hinged flaps aerodynamically boosted the retraction of the main gear. A simpler mechanical linkage eventually replaced the original hydraulic door flap; versions of it serve the various F-5 models as well.[19]

Round Two

F-5As, F-5Bs, and T-38s shared a high degree of commonality. The

F-5C designation was reserved for single-seat F-5A offshoots first tested in combat in Southeast Asia by the U.S. Air Force under the Skoshi Tiger project. Photos of F-5s in Vietnam show some data blocks listing F-5A; others are marked F-5C. Similarly, F-5D nomenclature was at one time intended for two-seat F-5B variants also envisioned for Skoshi Tiger.[20] Some Canadian-built two-seaters were occasionally designated CF-5D, with the letter signifying "Dual," as noted by aircraft researcher Joe Baugher. The next F-5s produced at Northrop were the significantly different F-5E and its two-seat F-5F counterpart, documented in Chapter 5.

Long before the debut of the improved F-5E, in the summer of 1965 Northrop tested an upgraded F-5A (63-8421) based on an airframe leased back from the U.S. Air Force. Initially called the F-5N (with the letter representing Northrop; later some upgraded F-5Es used by the Navy would carry the military designation F-5N), the company changed what it called the testbed to become the F-5A-15. The dash 15 referred to the uprated J85-15 engines used in this aircraft, which were rated at 4,300 lbs of thrust instead of 4,080 lbs produced by the J85-13 engines in production F-5As.

The experimental F-5A-15 incorporated design improvements including louvered auxiliary air inlet doors on the sides of the aft fuselage, just ahead of the engines. The doors, operated electrically, gave the engines more airflow for takeoff. They were designed to close automatically once the aircraft achieved a speed of 285 knots. The F-5A-15 also featured a two-position nosewheel strut. When lengthened, it gave the aircraft a three-degree nose-up attitude,

Three aspects of YF-5A 94989 photographed 15 February 1965 show the jet fitted with a centerline fuel tank plus white LAU-3 and -10 launchers interchangeably on underwing pylons. (AFFTC/HO collection)

YF-5A 989 cruised over the Mojave Desert, probably at the beginning of an ordnance dropping test sortie. Protrusion on lower side of nose near "U" of "U.S. Air Force" is a likely housing for an aft-looking camera to record stores separation details. (AFFTC/HO collection)

enhancing wing angle of attack for takeoff. This feature was said to reduce takeoff runs by as much as 25 percent. The strut could be lowered to provide better pilot visibility during taxiing.[21]

The company-sponsored F-5A-15 proved design concepts that were incorporated into production F-5s for years to come. Canadian CF-5As and CF-5Bs and others used the auxiliary air doors and the two-position nosewheel strut, which also surfaced on later F-5As as well as the bulked-up F-5E and F-5F.

Assembly Line Convenience

In keeping with its company philosophy to make the F-5 simple and accessible for its future maintainers, Northrop also devised an assembly line at its Hawthorne, California, plant that similarly facilitated production. The company was so proud of the line that it took out a two-page advertisement in Aviation Week & Space Technology to describe it, with text and photos that revealed construction aspects of the T-38 and F-5. The line held fuselages off the floor where access was easy. Northrop's ad text said: "...you couldn't take advantage of this 'airborne' assembly technique unless you had already designed your airframe so things can be put in easily from the outside after the skin is on.

"Northrop's T-38 and F-5 family of supersonic trainers and tactical fighters are designed so everything that needs maintaining is easy to get at. This means that the systems and subsystems are easy to install in the first place," the advertisement explained. Northrop said the easy accessibility to airframes under construction helped to make the resulting F-5s and T-38s "even more trouble-free by removing inconveniences that cause human beings to make mistakes." The text continued: "...the fuselages hang from elevated rails instead of resting on dollies. Sides of the fuselages are at natural standing height. Bottoms are far enough off the floor so men can work under them comfortably seated. The rails support platforms for work on top."

YF-5A 94989 carried a centerline-mounted SUU20A training bomb dispenser during testing at Edwards Air Force Base. (AFFTC/HO collection)

This sleek silver-painted F-5A without insignia, and identified only as "Viking" on photo documentation, was part of the Norwegian contract. (AFFTC/HO collection)

As fuselages needed to move to the next workstation on the assembly line, two people could push each rail-suspended fuselage to the next station. For the complexities of outfitting each cockpit, the forward fuselage sections hung in trunnions on their own assembly line before being mated to the center fuselages. In the trunnions, the forward fuselages could be rotated on their sides to simultaneously afford easy standing-height access to the cockpit cavities as well as the undersides of the structure.

Northrop said this assembly line technique was perfect for the F-5 series—large aircraft would be too big, and short production runs of other aircraft would make such a set-up too costly. "The T-38 and F-5, however, belong to a new generation. Their design carries sophistication to its logical end: simplicity. They deliver outstanding performance, yet they're simple to fly, simple to support and maintain. And with Northrop innovations in volume production techniques, they're simple to manufacture, too. We always wanted to build airplanes this way. Now we can."

If the company text sounds glowing, it nonetheless reveals and reinforces Northrop's self-identity as a seeker of simplicity, a recurring theme in the F-5 story.

Called NORAIL, for Northrop Overhead Rail Assembly and

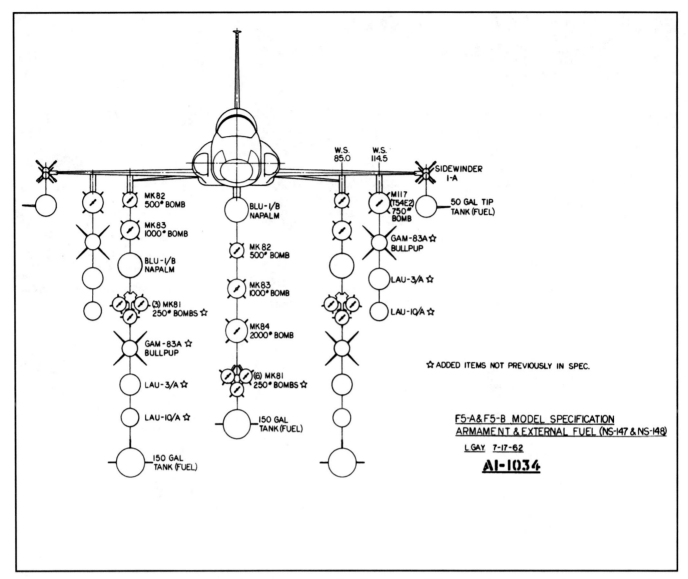

Detailed head-on drawing shows array of ordnance and fuel tanks that could be carried on F-5A and F-5B wing and centerline stations, circa July 1962. (Craig Kaston collection)

Two F-5Bs and an F-5A prepared for takeoff from Williams Air Force Base, Arizona, in the 1960s. (Air Force via Challen "Choni" Irvine)

Left side view of YF-5A 94989 shows clean airframe with wingtip missile rails installed, as photographed 29 July 1963. (AFFTC/HO collection)

Small size and ease of disassembly of the original N-156F (59-4987) facilitated its movement and storage in 1980 until the Museum of Flight's permanent location in Seattle was ready to place it on display.

Fuel tanks and a pair of Bullpup air-to-ground missiles on the outboard underwing pylons make up the load for an F-5A during the test program at Edwards Air Force Base. (AFFTC/HO collection)

Installation Line, the system used for building F-5s and T-38s at Northrop's Hawthorne, California, plant was developed by a team under Bob Lloyd, then Northrop's director of manufacturing engineering. Its twin assembly lines added up to 1,600 feet long, and simultaneously accommodated T-38s, F-5As, and F-5Bs. It deliberately capitalized on the celebrated ease of access designed into the three aircraft models. Aircraft mostly assembled at Hawthorne were shipped overland to Northrop's Palmdale, California, facility where main assemblies were mated to make complete aircraft. Over the years of F-5 and T-38 production, Palmdale established another NORAIL system for the F-5/T-38 series to perform some sub-assembly as well as final assembly, helping to ease production burdens on the Hawthorne plant.[22]

The use of an ergonomically thoughtful assembly line to build ergonomically thoughtful airplanes was much more than coincidence at Northrop; tooling and manufacturing experts were included in preliminary design discussions of the T-38 to optimize the design's producibility.

The first Freedom Fighter flew variously with its nose painted silver or black, although it did not carry radar. Orange DayGlo panels on the vertical fin and outer wing sections were used during test program. Photo taken 27 November 1963. (AFFTC/HO collection)

The third Freedom Fighter, later YF-5A 59-4989, was parked outdoors at the Air Force Museum near Dayton, Ohio, when photographed in October 1974. (Photo by Carl M. Johnsen)

The original N-156F Freedom Fighter looked like this on display in the delightfully crowded original museum of the Pacific Northwest Aviation Historical Foundation in Seattle near the Space Needle in November 1973.

Supersonic Summary

The ultimate F-5E and F-models are detailed in a later chapter of this book. The numbers of all models built illustrates the success of the Freedom Fighter concept. Northrop Grumman tallied construction of more than 2,600 F-5s, including those produced in cooperative agreements with Canada, the Republic of China (Taiwan), South Korea, Spain, and Switzerland. It is estimated that nearly two-thirds of all F-5s were still active in 2005. A decade earlier, the U.S. Air Force chose Northrop Grumman to manufacture 14 key structural elements and replacement parts to keep the international F-5 fleet viable. This program includes new wings, upper and lower cockpit longerons, horizontal stabilizers, some fuselage bulkheads, dorsal longerons, and engine inlet duct skin.[23]

As increasing numbers of F-5 users acquired F/A-18s, F-16s, and other fighters, the utility of the many surviving F-5s began to shift from primary fighter to lead-in trainer. Northrop offered a variety of parts and services to help users realize the lead-in trainer role for their F-5s. Northrop even offered to build new F-5F forward fuselage sections to modify single-seat F-5Es into two-place lead-in training aircraft.[24]

FOREIGN 2 CLIENTS

To serve the U.S. Military Assistance Program (MAP), about 170 F-5s, including around 18 two-seat B-models, were ordered early in the program. These were to help equip the air arms of South Korea, Greece, and Iran. Norway and Spain soon followed.[25] By 1974, Northrop counted 20 countries flying more than 1,100 F-5As and Bs. The initial F-5 nickname, Freedom Fighter, said it all: This was an aircraft for countries deemed vital in the global fight for freedom from communist domination. Changes in regimes over the decades have seen some countries move from friend to foe, or foe to friend. Users of the F-5 include, alphabetically:

Austria

Sometimes overlooked as a user of Northrop F-5s, Austria leased a number of F-5Es from Switzerland. These were said to be assigned to Austria's 2. Staffel of Uberwachungsgeschwader as of this writing. Ultimately, Austria chose the EF2000 Eurofighter to meet its 21st Century fighter requirements.[26]

Bahrain

In the mid 1980s, a decade after the creation of a Bahrain independent of British presence, a squadron of F-5Es with some F-5Fs gave the tiny Middle Eastern nation a viable fighter defense force. The country's 6th Fighter Squadron is said to operate the F-5s, while two

Canadian single-seat CF-5s like this example were sometimes fitted with a camera nose, said to be easier to swap with the regular fighter nose than was the installation on Northrop factory-built RF-5As.

Landing roll for a Canadian CF-5A on 21 July 1984 keeps elevators deflected and the nosewheel up for the braking benefits of increased drag. (Photo by Sharon Lea Johnsen)

other Royal Bahraini Air Force fighter squadrons fly F-16s. The F-5s sometimes serve as stepping-stones for pilots to transition into the F-16s.

Botswana

Botswana's Defence Force Air Wing acquired 10 ex-Canadian F-5As and three dual-place models

CF-5As stayed close with a Canadian Air Force 707 multi-use tanker. When fitted with refueling probes, the Canadian Freedom Fighters would fly to Europe in the escort of one of the 707s. CF-5 pilots sometimes found the refueling hose from the tanker's wingtip pods would gyrate in the vortex, making it a difficult target to engage with the refueling probe. With the necessity to refuel over the cold North Atlantic urgent, some CF-5 fliers would allow the refueling hose and basket assembly to strike the nose of the fighter to break the cycle of the vortex long enough to permit a quick coupling to take place. CF-5s sometimes bore dented noses as evidence of this overwater expedient. (Canadian Air Force photo)

(Canadian Freedom Fighters sometimes are called CF-116s, which in Botswana are designated CF-5s) in 1996; five more (including another pair of two-seaters) were delivered in 2000.[27]

Brazil

Interdiction and air superiority were two missions cited for Brazil's F-5Es and F-5Fs in the mid 1970s. Brazilian F-5s can be fitted for aerial refueling, using the country's KC-130 and KC-137 tanker aircraft. A few F-5Bs initially acquired by Brazil were supplanted in 1988 by F-models, along with additional F-5Es. Brazil's first batch of F-5Es used an extended dorsal fin to house antennas not

Canadian Freedom Fighters were popular guests at air shows in Canada as well as American venues like Paine Field, Washington, in July 1984. Three CF-5s fill the image with busy activity in a tight formation takeoff for the air show crowd. (Photo by Sharon Lea Johnsen)

found on the second batch, which were former USAF aggressor squadron aircraft.

Brazil's B-models were removed from service by the end of 1996.

Canada

An early customer of F-5s in 1968, Canada concluded its 27-year use of the Freedom Fighter in 1995.

Canadair built the 135 Canadian Freedom Fighters under license. Before Canada selected the F-5 for quantity purchase, the Canadian government considered the Grumman A-6A and Ling-Temco-Vought A-7A as contenders.

F-5As and F-5Bs employed several nomenclatures throughout their association with the Canadian Air Force. Generally called CF-5, the type in Canada has also been labeled the CF-116 in some documents. The Canadian two-seat aircraft, essentially B-models, have sometimes been identified as the CF-5D (Dual).

In addition to the use of a two-position nosewheel strut and auxiliary engine air doors in the aft fuselage, Canadian F-5s added a bird-proof windscreen, computing gunsight, and increased rudder authority. During the definition of Canadian F-5 requirements, the value of incorporating a Central Air Data Computer (CADC) became evident. (CADCs were becoming popular in the 1960s for their ability to process information about an aircraft's airspeed, altitude, and other parameters vital to optimal operation. The big Lockheed C-141A Starlifter, first flown in December 1963, was an operational CADC pioneer.) The availability of a CADC would prove crucial to the maneuver flap system of the F-5E and F-5F.

Flown as an adversary in Canadian training, this CF-5D (Dual) used a fake painted cockpit canopy on its belly. When banked abruptly, the presence of a bogus second canopy made it more difficult to quickly determine which way the fighter was banking, and turning. The paint scheme was photographed in 1979; aircraft is from 419 Squadron based at Cold Lake, Alberta, at the time.

A quartet of Canadian CF-5D (Dual) Freedom Fighters in 1983 shows the use of air-to-air missile rails on the wingtips of three of the two-seaters.

Some Canadian F-5s carried wraparound camouflage, as photographed in 1984.

Canadian Air Force CF-5A photographed in July 1984 carried detachable refueling probe on right side of the fuselage, unlike the pioneering Skoshi Tiger F-5Cs, which had the probe mounted on the left.

Chile

Chile operates dorsal-finned F-5Es and F-models as the "Tigre III" in Grupo de Aviacion No. 7. Local Chilean aviation industry, known as ENAER, has performed F-5E upgrades.

Ethiopia

The freedom-fighting stance of Ethiopian Emperor Haile Selassie was legendary ever since he battled invading Italian forces on the cusp of World War II. In 1966, Selassie's Ethiopian Air Force received a squadron of F-5As supported by a pair of two-seat F-5Bs.

Northrop documented the delivery of three Ethiopian F-5As by USAF pilots. The journey from the depot at McClellan AFB, near Sacramento, California, to Ethiopia involved 31 flying hours and 18 enroute stops. Four times, the diminutive fighters stopped to refuel as they crossed the United States eastbound. They could have carried more fuel in underwing drop tanks, but the trip was planned for shorter legs of 1-1/2 to 2 hours duration. For the journey, each F-5A was fitted with a centerline fuel tank plus the normal area-rule wingtip tanks.

From Goose Bay, Labrador, the jets crossed the cold North Atlantic, stopping at Greenland, Iceland, and Scotland. At Ramstein Air Base, Ger-

Banking Canadian Freedom Fighter exaggerates the prominence of the bent refueling probe in this 1984 photo.

Canadian CF-5A eased into the sky. Soon, during the main gear retraction cycle, metal flaps on the main gear doors would aerodynamically help boost the doors, and the gear, into closing more quickly than on hydraulic power alone.

many, a USAF T-39 Sabreliner joined the group as a mother ship, carrying officers familiar with European and Middle Eastern navigation and bureaucratic issues. The T-39 led the F-5s through Italy, Greece, Turkey, Iran, Saudi Arabia, and over the Red Sea to Ethiopia. The silver F-5As carried temporary U.S. star-and-bar insignia but were devoid of typical USAF markings.

Emperor Selassie's overthrow in 1974 by forces described as Marxist temporarily halted F-5 supplies from the United States, although attrition may have been compensated with ex-Iranian F-5s during this time. But interest in

Canadian CF-5 number 116831 carried a centerline training bomb dispenser that partially obscured the fake canopy painted on the belly of the jet as an optical illusion. (AFFTC/HO collection)

access to Red Sea ports in Eritrea may have prompted the delivery of a small number of F-5Es to Ethiopia the next year.

As the Soviet Union began supporting the new Ethiopian government, pro-U.S. sources of F-5s dried up. In an ironic turn of events, it is possible the Ethiopians subsequently received more F-5As and E-models from communist Vietnam. These aircraft were remnants of the F-5s supplied by the U.S. to South Vietnam before its fall.

Greece

Greece's Hellenic Air Force was a user of F-5As, F-5Bs, and RF-5As, expanding its Freedom Fighter fleet in the 1980s before drawing down to replace these aircraft in the late 1990s.

Hunduras

Ten Honduran Air Force F-5Es and two F-models served that country beginning in the late 1980s. These followed by a couple of

Multi-hued CF-5D, flown solo from the front seat, was part of a Canadian air show routine when photographed in the summer of 1984.

decades American fighters in the post-World War II years that had included P-63s, P-38s, and F4Us.

Indonesia

Indonesia's extended dorsal fin F-5Es and F-5Fs came on duty circa 1980, replacing CAC-27 Sabre models. The country had operated fleets of American and Soviet-style

fighters in previous eras. Starting in 1995, Indonesian F-5s were given upgraded armament and navigation avionics in a program with Belgium's SABCA, with early aircraft modified in Belgium and later modifications undertaken in Indonesia.

Skadron Udara 14 is said to be the unit operating Indonesian F-5s on Java.[28]

F-5B 63-8445 carried various markings in the mid-to-late 1960s including Royal Canadian Air Force (RCAF) insignia and a large Canadian flag during a period when Northrop was courting Canadian business. (Northrop via Craig Kaston collection)

With its auxiliary engine air-inlet doors open on the aft fuselage, a Canadian CF-5D was perhaps a foot from the runway when photographed in July 1983.

Forward location of front cockpit on F-5B/CF-5D puts pilot well ahead of rotation point around mainwheels. (Photo by Sharon Lea Johnsen)

Iran

The F-5As and F-5Bs furnished to the Shah of Iran for his country's air force in 1965 replaced F-84s in strike duties. Ultimately, Iran operated more than 100 A-models and more than 20 B-models.

Iran became the first country using F-5Es in 1974, buying more than 180 F-5Es, F-models, and RF-5Es. With the advent of F-5Es, Iran sold most of its F-5As to countries like Greece, Turkey, South Vietnam, Ethiopia, and Jordan. After the Shah's government fled Iran in January 1979, subsequent regimes were ultimately embargoed from receiving American aircraft and parts, so the F-5s of the now-Islamic Republic of Iran Air Force suffered increasing out-of-service rates. Ultimately, the indigenous Iranian aircraft industry managed to keep a number of F-5s airworthy.

Work said to be performed in Iran has included the conversion of F-5As to essential B-model configuration, and the possible reverse engineering of the F-5E by an ever-more capable Iranian industry.[29] Iranian F-5s are said to have been victorious in numerous engagements with Iraqi aircraft during disputes between the two countries (see F-5 Victory Claims heading at the end of this chapter).

Jordan

In the 1970s, Jordan's King Hussein juggled the intricacies of varied demographics within his country, the ever-present potential for confrontation with Israel, and a desire to maintain useful relations with the United States. Not an oil-producing country, Jordan had to rely on other means of ensuring its prosperity. In this political climate, Jordan was able

to receive about 30 F-5As and a smaller number of B-model Freedom Fighters cast off by the Imperial Iranian Air Force in 1974 and 1975 when Iran obtained newer F-5 Tiger II models.

In 1975, the Royal Jordanian Air Force took delivery of upgraded F-5Es and F-models from the U.S. In the early 1980s, a number of Jordanian F-5As and F-5Bs were transferred to Greece. Early Freedom Fighters sometimes wore the markings of several nations during their service lives.

Kenya

Kenya has been the operator of 10 to 12 F-5E/F models since 1978.[30] Kenyan F-5s feature the enlarged dorsal fin and an optional reconnaissance nose kit. They were given a camouflage scheme Northrop called African Jungle.

Libya

American relations with Libya since the late 1960s exemplify the intricacies of Middle East foreign policy. Eight F-5As and two F-5Bs were delivered to Libya in 1968 when the country was a monarchy under King Idris. Arab nations were recovering from the effects of the 1967 war with Israel. Pan-Arab sentiment and a perception of American support of Israel made it prudent for the United States to cultivate relationships with interested Arab countries.

The overthrow of King Idris in September 1969 and assumption of power by Col. Moamar Gaddafi changed the political tilt of Libya, and another eight F-5s earmarked for that country were withheld. The United States relinquished Wheelus Air Base and terminated a training program for Libyan F-5 pilots.

Gray F-5E served with the Royal Thai Air Force when photographed in the Philippines in January 1983.

Four Ethiopian F-5As held a snappy echelon formation. Ethiopia received F-5s in 1966. (Craig Kaston collection)

American instructors were said to be impressed by the capabilities of their Libyan students in-country and at Williams AFB, Arizona. Nonetheless, one Libyan F-5 was lost in the first three years of Libyan service, possibly the result of disorientation during a night mission over the Mediterranean Sea. A second Libyan F-5 was damaged by

Clean Norwegian F-5A carries numerals 13368 on tail, possibly shortened from serial number 64-13368, identified as an F-5A-20-NO. (AFFTC/HO collection)

F-5As of the Taiwanese air force held a finger-four formation. (Northrop via Craig Kaston collection)

F-5B 63-8445 alternately wore USAF markings and Canadian roundels circa 1966–'67 as Canada embraced the Freedom Fighter. The B-model was photographed in American markings at the Renton, Washington, air show in 1966. (Photo by Peter M. Bowers)

1970 in a runway mishap characterized as cartwheeling, in which the major damage sustained was a demolished vertical fin when the aircraft rolled.[31]

The Freedom Fighters in Libyan service were soon cut off from American aid, but it is reported these F-5s were kept flyable with assistance from Greek personnel. Libya also sent air force students to Pakistan to learn to fly, and it is possible Libyan F-5s were made available to Pakistan temporarily during hostilities with India in 1971. By the mid-1970s, with Libya increasingly cut off from sources of supply, seven of their F-5s may have been given to Turkey.[32]

Malaysia

Malaysia ordered F-5Es, Fs, and RF-5E Tigereye recon jets. By the early 21st century, Malaysian F-5s had been placed in storage, although some were subsequently returned to flying status.

Mexico

Mexican air force F-5Es with extended dorsal fin antenna housings continue to serve in limited numbers as this book is written. Mexico took delivery of about a dozen E- and F-models, probably in the ratio of 10 F-5Es to two F-5Fs.

Morocco

As American relations with the government of Morocco improved in the late 1960s, Morocco received two squadrons of F-5As supported by a small number of B-models for training. Moroccan F-5s participated in a failed coup attempt against King Hassan II on 16 August 1972, when several of the jets attacked the

Boeing 727 carrying King Hassan. Though damaged, the 727 made an emergency landing, whereupon the airfield was reportedly strafed by one of the F-5s. Four F-5s unsuccessfully attacked the Moroccan royal palace that day.

Fighting between factions who wanted former Spanish Sahara territory after Spain withdrew in 1974 threatened a peaceful partitioning of the area planned by Morocco and Mauritania. Moroccan F-5s flew air-to-ground sorties in an effort to quell the problem, reportedly losing F-5s to SA-7 surface-to-air missiles. F-5Es subsequently bolstered the reduced Moroccan F-5 inventory.[33]

The Netherlands

Canadair, in addition to manufacturing Canada's Freedom Fighters, built 105 A- and B-models for the Royal Netherlands Air Force. The breakout was said to include 75 single-seat A-models and 30 F-5Bs when the order was placed with Canadair in early 1967. Fokker was set to build wings and other parts to be sent to Canada for inclusion in the Dutch F-5 production run. The Dutch F-5s replaced or augmented F-84Fs, F-104Gs, and in the training role, T-33s. The Dutch government earlier had contemplated a joint Dutch-Belgian buy of 221 F-5s, to be built in The Netherlands and Belgium, but this plan did not bear fruit.[34]

Dutch F-5s introduced enlarged wing tanks, and single-position maneuvering flaps, for better combat maneuvering.

Norway appreciated the Northrop philosophy of creating a less-expensive aircraft alternative to the Norwegians' costly F-104G Starfighters. An early NATO (North Atlantic Treaty Organization)

Brazilian F-5E was photographed with enlarged dorsal fin visible. (Northrop via Craig Kaston collection)

Indonesian air force F-5Es with enlarged dorsal fins used blue-gray variegated camouflage scheme. (Craig Kaston collection)

Missile-equipped F-5F and F-5E represented Singapore. (Northrop via Craig Kaston collection)

customer of F-5s, the Royal Norwegian Air Force first received F-5As in the summer of 1965.

Northrop documentation initially identified Norway's Freedom Fighters as F-5A(G)s. To accommodate cold weather conditions and short landing fields, the Norwegian F-5s were distinguished at that time by features including laminated electrically heated anti-ice windscreens fit within the standard F-5A frame. Norwegian Freedom Fighters were also designed to employ a cast aluminum engine inlet lip with an electric heating blanket and a temperature controller. Short field operations were to be accommodated by the instal-lation of JATO rocket racks for four jettisonable 16N5-1000 JATO bottles capable of giving 4,000 lbs of thrust for takeoff. And an arresting hook was devised, requiring beefed-up structure to withstand a shock of 56,250 lbs.[35]

The equivalent of six squadrons–more than 70 aircraft–made up Norway's F-5A and B-model force. Some were obtained by purchase, others through the U.S. Military Assistance Program. The rigors of flying over Norway led to attrition and wear and tear, but upgrades and rebuilds kept the Norwegian Freedom Fighters going. Their replacement in Norwegian service has been the F-16.

Philippines

A 1966 recipient of 22 Freedom Fighters, the Philippine air force even established a jet demonstration team, the Blue Diamonds, flying F-5s. The 1960s were good years for the Philippine Air Force, with new F-5s serviced by American-trained personnel. In 1968, six F-5As comprised the Blue Diamonds. By the mid 1970s, energy problems and insurgent issues took a toll on the availability of the Filipino F-5 team.

Filipino F-5s occasionally saw combat in their own country against factions threatening the status quo. In November 1972, rebels on Sibalu Hill in Sulu were close to annihilating a Filipino marine battalion trapped in rebel-held territory. Airpower was massed, and the following morning fighters including F-5s flew repeated sorties against the rebels, thwarting their attack on the marines and permitting helicopters to rescue the men.

In 1989, Filipino F-5 pilots loyal to the government disabled aircraft used by rebel forces including a handful of armed T-28s and at least one Sikorsky helicopter at Sangley Field. The original contingent of Filipino F-5s was boosted at least once in 1998 with the acquisition of five F-5s from

Triangle-emblazoned F-5E and F-5F of the air force of Mexico featured enlarged dorsal fins and wraparound jungle camouflage. (Northrop via Craig Kaston collection)

Striking camouflage pattern of the Imperial Iranian Air Force covered F-5E 73-00933. (Northrop via Craig Kaston collection)

F-5E in desert camouflage scheme that extends to brown missiles on the wingtips belonged to the air force of Morocco. (Northrop via Craig Kaston collection)

Korea. By the early 1990s, only about 10 Filipino F-5As and Bs were said to be airworthy.

According to Filipino sources, the last of that country's Freedom Fighters were retired in October 2005.

Portugal

Portugal's air force at one time included about a dozen T-38 Talons. The T-38s are said to be the first jets in Portuguese service to attain the speed of sound in level flight. They served from 1977 to 1993. Several have been preserved in Portugal.

Saudi Arabia

In the summer of 1964, six Saudi Arabian army and air force personnel traveled to the U.S. air base in Wiesbaden, Germany, to evaluate the early F-5. The Saudi evaluation was to be followed by Northrop visits to Iran, Libya, Greece, Turkey, Italy, Portugal, and Spain later that year.[36]

The advent of the inertial navigation system (INS) was hailed as a precision wonder in the years before satellite global positioning became available. Saudi Arabia

The traveling F-5B (63-8445) wore Canadian markings when photographed at Abbotsford, British Columbia, in August 1967; other photos show this same blue-topped Freedom Fighter in U.S. markings a year earlier.

Two Saudi F-5Es refueled simultaneously from a Saudi Arabian KC-130 Hercules transport/tanker. (Northrop via Craig Kaston collection)

Slow-speed auxiliary inlet louver doors were still open when this Swiss air force F-5E was photographed. (Northrop via Craig Kaston collection)

desired inclusion of INS in its F-5s to avoid border overflights in the sensitive Middle East. This customer request provided an opportunity for Northrop, working with Litton, to replace the older attitude and heading reference system (AHRS) on the F-5.

Singapore

Singapore has the distinction of receiving the last F-5E built (86-0409), said to be assembled from spare parts even after the Northrop line was officially closed down. The small size of Singapore masks its financial strength, and its ability to maintain a viable air force. An operator of F-5Es, RF-5Es, and F-5Fs, the Republic of Singapore Air Force commissioned a modernization program for these jets in the mid 1990s. Singapore Technologies Aerospace, assisted by Elbit of Israel, did the work, and the refreshed Singapore F-5s are designated F-5S for single-seaters and F-5T for two-place versions. Improved fire-control radar and other upgraded avionics are central to the modifications.[37]

Chilean F-5E was painted in mottled gray camouflage. (Northrop via Craig Kaston collection)

South Korea

Long considered a bulwark against potential communist threats in the Far East, the Republic of Korea (ROK) has employed several American fighter systems in its air force, including several models of the F-5 series. F-5A Freedom Fighters were introduced in April 1965; F-5Es and F-models came to South Korea in November 1974. The last remaining ROK F-5As and Bs were retired by August of 2005.[38]

South Korean industry participated in the construction and assembly of some ROK F-5Es and Fs. Korean Tiger IIs were fitted with teardrop radar warning receivers (RWR) on both sides of the fuselage near the nose and tail, as were the later F-5s of a number of countries.

Spain

In the first part of 1965, Spain signed up to buy 70 F-5As and B-models for its air force. Sometimes identified as SF-5s, the aircraft were built under license by Construcciones Aeronauticas, S.A. (CASA) in Spain.

Three years after first buying F-5s, Spain announced a requirement for a radar-equipped jet interceptor in 1968. This served as impetus for Northrop, working with Emerson, to devise radar for the F-5. Although Spain ultimately picked the French Mirage for the radar interceptor role, the radar developmental work accomplished on F-5s became the basis for the successful radar carried by the later F-5E.[39]

Sudan

Sudan began using F-5Es and Fs (probably seven single-seaters and a pair of two-seaters) in 1981.

Switzerland

The Swiss Air Force gained 85 F-5 Tiger IIs in 1978. In addition to tactical use, Swiss F-5s formed a jet demonstration team. Swiss Tiger IIs were fitted for chaff and flare dispensing, and with handling qualities refinements including the flattened sharknose and enlarged W-6 LEX (leading edge extension). Radar warning receivers (RWR) were installed.

With F/A-18s on the ascendancy in Switzerland into 2005, a number of ex-Swiss F-5Es, now called F-5Ns, were introduced into the U.S. Navy's VFC-13 dissimilar combat aircraft training squadron at Naval Air Station Fallon, Nevada.

Taiwan

Taiwan—Nationalist China—has been a Northrop customer since F-5A and B-model days. This small island nation off the coast of the People's Republic of China arrays most of its airfields nearest that coastal side of the island; traditional tensions between the two nations are evident. Taiwan's F-5 force has been as high as 283 of the fighters around 1990; 90 are expected to remain in service until around 2015 or later.

Later batches of Taiwanese Tiger IIs were fitted with flare/chaff dispensers, the handling qualities upgrades (enlarged LEX and sharknose), and radar warning receivers (RWR).

Thailand

The value of air bases in Thailand was significant to American efforts in Southeast Asia in the last half of the 1960s and into the early 1970s. As the Thai government accommodated U.S. warplanes based within its borders, the Thai Air Force became the recipient in 1966 of two squadrons of mostly F-5As, with a few RF-5As and at least two F-5Bs. Subsequently, a couple additional F-5Bs were reported to have been acquired from Malaysia, and F-5Es were added to the Thai inventory.

Tunisia

Wedged between Algeria and Libya on the North African Mediterranean coast, Tunisia has a

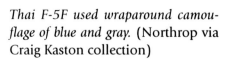

Two Tunisian F-5Fs rolled away from the camera, revealing black-and-white ringed arresting hooks. (Northrop via Craig Kaston collection)

Thai F-5F used wraparound camouflage of blue and gray. (Northrop via Craig Kaston collection)

South Korea operated late-model Northrops like this gray F-5F after years of flying F-5As and B-models. (Northrop via Craig Kaston collection)

Three silver F-5As released finless napalm canisters over Luke Air Force Base's North South TAC range in Arizona in the 1960s. (Challen Irvine collection)

squadron of F-5Es and F-models with the enlarged dorsal fin carrying antennas.

Turkey

Another user of Northrop T-38 Talons, as this book is written, Turkey also flies upgraded F-5As and Bs, especially as lead-in training for Turkish F-16 pilots. The precision team Turkish Stars flies F-5s. More than 200 F-5s are said to have served the Turkish Air Force over the years.

Venezuela

Venezuelan use of the F-5 includes the purchase of 20 retired CF-5s from Canada. CF-5s upgraded by Singapore Technologies Aerospace for Venezuela have been called VF-5As and VF-5Bs. Some former Dutch NF-5s supplanted Canadian Freedom Fighters in Venezuela.

Vietnam

Vietnam's association with the F-5 series spans the war years, when the Republic of Vietnam—South Viet-

nam—flew F-5As, Bs, and later variants against communist opposition, and the subsequent absorption of remaining F-5 assets when North Vietnam took over the south. In 1962 and into 1963, American military planners contemplated equipping some South Vietnamese Air Force squadrons with F-5s by 1966. The U.S. Air Force brought the first F-5s to Vietnam.

In January 1966, C. M. Plattner, an engineering editor for *Aviation Week & Space Technology* magazine, published a tally of U.S. Air Force aircraft in South Vietnam that included 11 F-5As.[40] This was the core of a dozen F-5As flown by U.S. Air Force pilots in a combat evaluation of the Freedom Fighter.

By early August 1966, the U.S. Air Force contemplated buying 95 more F-5s, some of which would equip South Vietnamese Air Force squadrons. Proposed was a 90-gallon dorsal fuel tank addition.[41]

Before the collapse of South Vietnam, F-5Es were ordered and painted in jungle camouflage. Some of these aircraft later went to South Korea and American aggressor units when they were collected in Thailand as South Vietnamese pilots fled their country with the war's end.

The gear is almost up as a Canadian CF-5A takes off at an American air show near Everett, Washington, on 21 July 1984. Angle shows negative dihedral of horizontal stabilizers. (Photo by Sharon Lea Johnsen)

Canadair supplied NF-5s like this B-model to the Netherlands, constructed in Canada with an infusion of Dutch-made parts. (Canadair photo)

Malaysian RF-5E Tigereye on turn to final approach shows ability to carry air-to-air missiles in addition to discharging a sophisticated reconnaissance mission. Fairing on belly near wing trailing edge is chaff/flare dispenser. (Northrop via Craig Kaston collection)

Stories indicate some former South Vietnamese F-5As and Es were flown by the Vietnamese People's Air Force after the 1975 fall of the Saigon government. It is reported that at least two captured South Vietnamese F-5s were sent to the Eastern bloc countries of Czechoslovakia and Poland for evaluation.[42]

Yemen Arab Republic

The Yemen Arab Republic, which includes the former North Yemen, used ex-Saudi F-5Bs and later F-5Es. Some are believed to have remained serviceable at least as late as 2000.

Others

Some evidence suggests that Pakistan was the beneficiary of a few

Libyan F-5s sent to that country ostensibly for training during a time when hostilities flared between Pakistan and India in the 1970s. The possibility exists that Pakistan acquired a handful of surplus Iranian F-5s in the early 1970s before sending them to Greece.[43]

F-5 Victory Claims

In the decades since F-5s first graced the air forces of countries around the globe, they have participated in aerial combat a number of times. A compilation of F-5 aerial victory claims includes:

• Ethiopia (flown by Israeli pilots): 7 victories vs. Somalia, 1977
• North Yemen: 5 victories vs. South Yemen, 1994.
• Iran: 23 victories vs. Iraq, (1980s).
• Thailand: 1 victory vs. Vietnam (helicopter), 1980s.
• Greece: Some probable victories vs. Turkey, mid 1970s.

F-5s have been lost in aerial combat too; the F-5 win-loss ratio is said to be about 4-1.[44]

When a coalition of countries went to war with Iraq during Oper-ation Desert Storm in January 1991, about 75 F-5s were included in the inventories of two air forces in the alliance. Bahrain had 12 F-5Es; Saudi Arabia had 53 F-5Es and F-models as well as 10 RF-5E single-seat reconnaissance fighters. One Saudi F-5 was reported as lost over Iraq on 13 February.[45]

Saudi RF-5Es, equipped with sophisticated optics, are said to have provided reconnaissance coverage over Kuwait when smoke from oilfield fires dimmed the effectiveness of other reconnaissance platforms.

Angled camera windows and presence of cannon are evident in side view of Malaysian RF-5E Tigereye in formation with single-engine Northrop F-20 Tigershark. (Northrop via Craig Kaston collection)

Festive red ribbon adorned the first F-5E delivered to Nationalist China. The Nationalist Chinese air force arrays its assets on the side of Taiwan that faces mainland communist China. (Northrop via Craig Kaston collection)

SKOSHI 3 TIGER

The U.S. Air Force, not a full-fledged operational customer for F-5s, nonetheless took a special squadron of Freedom Fighters into combat in Vietnam in 1965 as an extensive evaluation of the aircraft's capabilities. The premise was to compare F-5 operations with those of the F-4C, F-100, and F-104. The operational test was called Skoshi Tiger, the name generally associated with many aspects of this project.

The Skoshi Tiger aircraft were hybrids. Though sometimes called F-5As, these combat jets also are referenced in Air Force documentation as F-5Cs.[46] They incorporated fixed, angled refueling probes on the left side of the forward fuselage. They also added armor plate and jettisonable stores pylons. The rudder limiter was removed, and a new gyro system was installed. They carried an Air Force-style Southeast Asia camouflage scheme.[47]

The in-flight refueling boom could be removed. Its MA-2 nozzle was compatible with the KC-135 tanker boom-to-drogue adapter kit.

The F-5 in-flight refueling system weighed 85 lbs; when the boom was removed, only three pounds additional airframe weight resulted from the boom modification. Refueling of internal and external tanks could be simultaneous, at a rate of 1,600 lbs of fuel a minute.[48]

Challen "Choni" Irvine, a veteran of early U.S. Air Force F-5 operations in the U.S., offered suggestions to Northrop that helped make the design of the refueling plumbing a fairly simple attachment through an existing fuel tank cleanout port.[49]

To fortify the F-5 against a hostile ground fire environment, 1/4-inch-thick face-hardened steel armor plate was mounted externally between fuselage stations 194.0 and 253.5 as well as between fuselage stations 483.0 and 537.75. The forward plates, below the cockpit, protected the pilot and the control mechanism. The aft plates protected vital hydraulic and control areas near the tail. The armor added 236 lbs to the weight of the Skoshi Tiger F-5A.[50]

All five pylon-stations were jettisonable on Skoshi Tiger F-5s. They incorporated explosive attaching bolts to accomplish this. A cam and J-hook fitted at the aft end of the pylon and quick disconnects for electric contacts, air, and fuel, helped assure clean separation from the aircraft when the pylon was jettisoned. Skoshi Tiger F-5s also used multiple ejector bomb racks to increase the stores carrying flexibility over that of contemporary F-5s.[51]

The Skoshi F-5s had modified throttle linkage with improved afterburner modulation. According to an Air Force description, this change "provided usable thrust control in the afterburner range for formation flight."[52]

The Skoshi Tiger F-5s enjoyed increased combat maneuverability due to the deletion of the rudder limiter. Standard F-5s of the time had a five-degree rudder stop imposed when the landing gear was up. With the additional rudder travel available to Skoshi Tiger F-5 pilots, hydraulic power to the rudder acti-

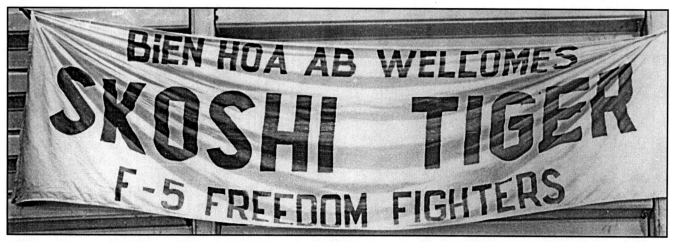

Skoshi Tiger F-5s and the men supporting them arrived in Vietnam with a banner welcoming them in October 1965. (AFHRA)

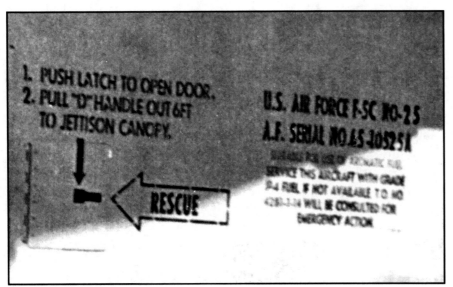

Close-up of data on a single-seat Freedom Fighter shows it is F-5C 65-10525A, equipped with a left-side refueling probe like the earlier original Skoshi Tiger machines. This Freedom Fighter almost certainly wound up as a South Vietnamese Air Force F-5. (Craig Kaston collection)

vators was reduced from 3,000 lbs per square inch (psi) to 1,500 psi in an effort to limit the available hinge moment to the rudder surface.[53]

To prevent precession (movement of heading and attitude indications) and to prevent tumbling of gyroscopic instrument readouts, as a result of anticipated combat maneuvers, a two-gyro platform (Displacement Gyro, Type SBK-1/A246-5, AERNO 60-1499) replaced the standard F-5 gyro (Type MP-1, AERNO 60-5937).[54]

Additional formation lights adorned the Skoshi Tiger aircraft.

And in view of their mission to quantify the F-5's combat suitability, the Skoshi Freedom Fighters were fitted with a VGH recorder to measure flight parameters.[55]

For four and a half months in 1965 and into 1966, these USAF F-5s totaled 2,600 sorties. A Northrop account says the USAF Freedom Fighters, operating under the project name Skoshi Tiger, achieved an operational readiness rate of 85 percent and an abort rate of 1.5 percent.

The official USAF history of Skoshi Tiger, subsequently declassified, describes the operation's

premise in terms that may reveal both the F-5's supporters goals as well as a sometimes-voiced USAF perception that the F-5 was too rudimentary for much of that service's requirements: "The history of project Skoshi Tiger covers the combat evaluation of a modified F-5A airplane – a relatively cheap, unsophisticated jet fighter, whose capabilities might prove beneficial in the lower levels of conflict." Skoshi Tiger was a project in a hurry, with a timetable that barely spanned parts of 1965 and 1966.[56]

By the spring of 1965, it was evident to American military planners that the U.S. Air Force inventory was comprised of aircraft envisioned for higher levels of conflict inconsistent with some of the needs of wars like that being fought in Southeast Asia. These sophisticated USAF warplanes had to be modified, in some instances, to render them suitable for lower-level conflicts. The Air Force's official Skoshi Tiger history notes: "A review of the functional performance characteristics of fighter aircraft of this class revealed that the Northrop-built F-5A might be the solution to reach this better balance in force structure."

Already undergoing evaluation at the Tactical Air Warfare Center at Eglin AFB, Florida, in a project called Sparrow Hawk, the F-5A seemed to fit the bill. Sparrow

Skoshi Tiger original-equipment F-5 number 63-8426 flies to a hostile target area in Southeast Asia in company with other Skoshi jets. Presence of refueling probe suggests this could be during the out-country phase of operations. (AFHRA)

Hawk was originally conceived to see if the Tactical Air Command (TAC) could benefit from the acquisition of a lightweight fighter. The Grumman A-6A, Douglas A-4E, and Northrop F-5A were initially considered for this TAC mission. The A-6 was subsequently withdrawn from consideration, and the A-4C replaced the E-model in Sparrow Hawk deliberations. On 1 May 1965, TAC recommended to the Air Force chief of staff that Project Sparrow Hawk be ended, with Sparrow Hawk F-5s earmarked for a combat evaluation in Vietnam. Because the F-5 was available as a Military Assistance Program (MAP) choice for use by American allies, access to a quantity of F-5s for a combat evaluation was deemed practical. A week later, USAF Headquarters advised TAC to make preliminary plans for supporting 12 F-5s in Vietnam by October of that year; by 18 May, USAF Headquarters was calling the project Skoshi Tiger. Earlier, it sometimes had been referenced as Sparrow Hawk II.[57]

Col. Frank N. Emory was tagged to command the Skoshi Tiger squadron; his deputy was Lt. Col. W. F. Georgi. At this stage in the planning, the total temporary duty commitment for the evaluation was estimated at approximately eight months. The objective was to determine the combat effectiveness of the F-5A in comparison with other fighter aircraft in the USAF inventory, and also flying in Southeast Asia. Colonel Emory's Skoshi Tiger squadron was activated as the 4503rd Tactical Fighter Squadron (Provisional) at Williams AFB, Arizona, on 26 July 1965. (Dates of organization and activation sometimes vary in Air Force lineage; suffice it to say, by the end of July 1965, Skoshi Tiger had a home.)

Eighteen pilots were assigned

Col. Frank N. Emory paused with one of the Skoshi Tiger Block-20 F-5As on the date he flew the unit's 1,000th combat sortie, 5 December 1965. This aircraft is identified as an A-model; the marking of Skoshi aircraft as C-models was not comprehensive. (AFHRA)

to the Skoshi Tiger squadron, affording a ratio of 1.5 pilots to each of the 12 F-5s. Additionally, the squadron's command section included some pilots who were checked out in F-5 operations, making at least 22 fliers available for Skoshi Tiger if needed. The pilots were carefully screened volunteers who had varying amounts of experience in the F-100, F-4, F-105, and F-104. Six already had F-100 combat experience in Southeast Asia and four were alumni of the original Sparrow Hawk evaluation at Eglin. To support Skoshi Tiger's Freedom Fighters, maintenance troops included a number of Sparrow Hawk veterans as well as other maintainers with previous T-38 and F-5 experience in the Air Training Command. When a higher headquarters decision was made to accelerate the squadron's operational readiness date from December to not later than 1 November 1965,

Skoshi Tiger went on a seven-day week, with 12-hour scheduled days.[58] Pilots assigned to Skoshi Tiger were trained at Williams AFB, starting on 2 August 1965, in five ex-Sparrow Hawk F-5s ferried from Eglin AFB. T-38s also provided eight to 10 hours of flying time for some of the Skoshi Tiger trainees. The training curriculum included briefings and flights intended to prepare the Skoshi Tiger pilots for the eventualities of air-to-air combat, originally offered as one goal of the overseas evaluation. The flight-training syllabus at Williams included AIM-9B firing for Skoshi pilots. During this time, Northrop modified 12 F-5As at its Palmdale, California, facility for the project, delivering them over a period of time between 17 September and 11 October. Skoshi Tiger F-5 serial numbers are: 63-8424, -8425, -8426, -8428, -8429, 64-13314, -13315, -13316, -13317, -13318, -13319, and -13332.[59]

F-5 Goes To War

The dozen Skoshi Tiger air-refuelable F-5Cs deployed to Southeast Asia from Williams AFB, Arizona, in a hop to Hickam AFB, Hawaii, on 20 October 1965, and departed the following day. The jazzy jets, in camouflage paint, drew interest from Air Force officials and media in Hawaii. Seven Strategic Air Command (SAC) KC-135 tankers supported the first leg of the F-5 deployment.[60] Call signs for the seven tankers on the leg from Hawaii to Guam were "Dwarf," calling to mind the adventures of Snow White.[61] The leg from Williams AFB to Hickam AFB covered 2,594 miles, lasting six hours with the aid of eight refuelings. The pioneering overwater Skoshi Tiger jets continued their trek from Hickam to Andersen AFB, Guam, with stops at Midway and Wake, plus five refuelings. The final journey to Bien Hoa, Vietnam, from Guam included a stop at Clark Air Base, Philippines, and required three more refuelings.[62] Nineteen Air Force transports, ranging from C-130s to C-124s and a C-135, moved Skoshi Tiger's personnel and equipment to Vietnam. Four hours after the Skoshi Tiger F-5s landed at Bien Hoa in Vietnam, two of the Freedom Fighters, piloted by Maj. Roy L. Holbrook, Jr. and Capt. James W. Thar, flew the unit's first combat sorties as they struck at a Viet Cong concentration estimated to be as high as 500 men in war zone D. The brace of F-5s each carried four 500-lb bombs and 500 rounds of 20-mm cannon ammunition for this inaugural mission. Each F-5 made five bomb runs and two strafing passes over the target, with no return fire noted. Thus began a regimen intended to log 50 hours a month for four months on each of the Skoshi Tiger F-5s.[63]

Fitted with centerline and underwing fuel tanks for the flight, a brace of Skoshi Tiger F-5s departed Bien Hoa for deployment to Da Nang as part of the F-5's combat evaluation. (AFHRA)

Skoshi Tiger settled into a series of sorties against ground targets. Through the end of December 1965, most of the F-5 missions were within 40 miles of home base. According to the official history of the squadron: "Many of these sorties were strikes against high priority, last-minute targets that ranged from Viet Cong troops to sampans, trucks, and dwellings. In many cases, these targets were assigned to the F-5 pilots after they were airborne and on the way to a scheduled pre-planned strike."

The only Skoshi F-5 lost to combat was believed to have been hit by ground fire during an attack mission about 15 miles west of Saigon on 16 December 1965. The Freedom Fighter was seen to catch fire at the beginning of a strafing pass following two napalm runs on the same target area. The pilot, Maj. Joseph B. Baggett, ejected and was rescued by an Army helicopter, but he died subsequently from injuries received.[64]

As the month ended, Skoshi Tiger counted 1,531 sorties making up 496 missions in Phase I of the combat test. Phase I saw Skoshi F-5s use 3,110,886 lbs of ordnance against Viet Cong targets. The official record for Skoshi Tiger claimed 1,377 structures destroyed, with another 1,292 structures damaged between the squadron's arrival in October and 30 December 1965. Additionally, 76 sampans were listed as destroyed by F-5s, with another 36 damaged. Fifty-nine secondary explosions were counted, and 132 Viet Cong were listed as killed, four wounded, and an additional 57 VC were estimated to have been killed in F-5 attacks.[65]

Skoshi Tiger F-5s deployed to a forward operating base at Da Nang for rigorous missions outside South Vietnam as Phase II of the evaluation. The purpose of this deployment was a calculated exposure of the F-5s to heavily defended targets in North Vietnam, with an increased likelihood of air-to-air combat over the north as well. But a presidential halt on bombing North Vietnam at that time caused a diversion of the Da Nang F-5s to hit targets in Laos, using air refueling to give sufficient range. During the period 3 to 30 January 1966,

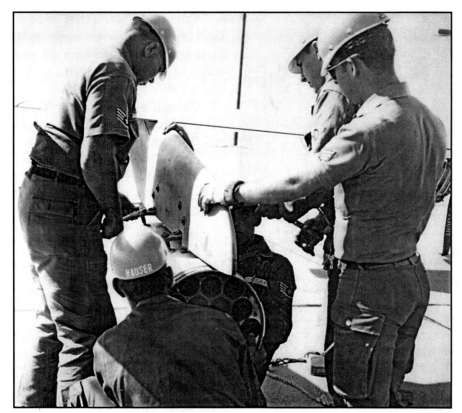

Mechanics mounted a 2.75-inch folding fin rocket launcher to an F-5 wing station. This may have been a training session at Williams AFB, Arizona, before Skoshi Tiger forces deployed to South Vietnam. (AFHRA)

Skoshi Tiger F-5s amassed 577:50 hours of flying time in 397 combat sorties. When a January three-day ceasefire to observe the Vietnamese Lunar New Year precluded F-5 sorties in Vietnam, the F-5s flew interdiction missions along Laotian portions of the Ho Chi Minh trail, knocking out bridges and cratering roads. The F-5 fliers were credited with the destruction of six bridges and the damaging of seven more during the 30-day deployment to Da Nang. They also detected and destroyed three fords used by the communists to cross streams. The fords were built just beneath the surface of the water, making it possible to cross the stream even as it flowed over the ford. The water's surface made the ford almost impossible to detect from the air. Occasionally, pilots would glimpse vehicle tracks leading to and from a stream with

no bridge evident—a telltale sign of a ford. Once focused on this evidence, the ford could sometimes be faintly discerned, enabling a successful F-5 attack.[66]

On 2 February 1966, Skoshi Tiger began Phase III of the F-5 combat evaluation with accelerated in-country missions flown from Bien Hoa for 10 days. The jets logged 348 combat sorties in this phase, spewing 51,749 rounds of 20-mm ammunition, firing 456 rockets, and dropping 376 BLU-1B napalm bombs, 54 CBU-2A canisters, 466 MK-82 bombs, and 428 M-117 bombs. The load carried by the F-5s during this phase averaged 2,603 lbs per sortie. The marauding Skoshi Tiger jets were credited, according to intelligence reports, with the destruction of 312 structures and the damaging of 245 more during Phase III. Twenty-six

bunkers were destroyed by the F-5s, and 21 sampans were sunk and eight more damaged. Four secondary explosions were noted during the Phase III F-5 attacks.[67]

Heading North

Denied a chance to fight over North Vietnam earlier, Skoshi Tiger's deployment in Vietnam was extended beyond its original return date of 20 February 1966 to allow a Phase IV out-country effort from Da Nang, following the lifting of the Christmas moratorium on bombing targets in North Vietnam. The Air Force Skoshi Tiger history documentation noted: "This appeared to be the last chance to evaluate the F-5 aircraft in the air defense environment of North Vietnam, as anticipated in the evaluation program. There was also the possibility that the aircraft might encounter communist MIG [sic] aircraft and this would be the acid test to determine the F-5's chances of survival in aerial combat with enemy aircraft. These were the contributing factors that led to the Hq USAF decision for extending the unit for another short period in the Republic of Vietnam."[68]

Out-country sorties began 22 February from Da Nang with weather dictating a reassignment of the F-5s to interdiction flights over Laos. The Phase IV plan called for Skoshi Tiger to mount 16 sorties daily against targets in either North Vietnam or Laos. Running until 9 March, the Skoshi Tiger jets logged 176 combat sorties on 45 missions over both North Vietnam and Laos for which they counted 374 flying hours. The F-5 pilots expended 5,923 rounds of 20-mm ammunition and 543 M-117 750-lb bombs on these out-country bombing and strafing sorties. Damage claims included

A bomb-laden Skoshi Tiger F-5 received maintenance attention in a steel revetment at Bien Hoa. High-walled revetments used in Vietnam diminished collateral damage if enemy mortar attacks hit parked aircraft. (AFHRA)

seven structures destroyed, three stream fords bombed, six trucks demolished, and two more trucks damaged. Two secondary explosions, sometimes a clue to the value of a target, were noted. Skoshi Tiger F-5s flew high-altitude escort and MiG combat air patrol missions during this time, armed with two AIM-9B missiles.[69] About one-fourth of the Phase IV out-country missions were in the role of air superiority fighter in northern Laos, providing a protective cap for fighter-bomber strikes and escorting high-altitude ELINT (electronic intelligence) aircraft. Overall, nearly half of the Phase IV F-5 missions were affected by weather conditions that caused the F-5s to be re-ordered to secondary or tertiary targets.[70]

Skoshi Tiger Statistics[71]

Missions 825
Sorties..2,664
(listed in the Skoshi Tiger final evaluation as 2,651)
Aborts 42
Sorties Cancelled 95

Ordnance Expended
BLU-1B (750-pound napalm) 2,295
CBU-2A 118
LAU-3 (launchers) 259
   (LAU-3 rockets fired) 4,918
20-mm (rounds fired) 614,193
MK-81 (250-pound bomb) 70
MK-82 (500-pound bomb) 2,210
MK-83 (1,000-pound bomb).........4
M-117 (750-pound bomb)......3,212

Mission Results
Killed by air action......................231
Estimated killed by air action 163
Wounded by air action 4
Structures destroyed 1,963
Structures damaged...................1,713
Sampans destroyed 105
Sampans damaged........................55
Secondary explosions 77
Fortifications destroyed 181
Missions unobserved 313
Trucks destroyed 7
Bridges destroyed 8
Fords bombed and destroyed 15
Barges destroyed.............................3

Curiously, different Skoshi Tiger reports show some variables in these figures; such statistics are best taken as an indication of activity levels, rather than irrefutable.

Though only one Skoshi Tiger F-5 was lost due to probable enemy action, numerous bullet holes were counted in Freedom Fighters returning from sorties. A running tally kept by the Air Force shows the following Skoshi Tiger F-5 battle damage:

28 October 1965: One .30-cal hole in top of vertical stabilizer.
11 November: One .50-cal hole in intake.
11 November: Two .30-cal holes – one in left tip tank and one in gun door.
16 November: One .30-cal hole in nose electronics compartment.
1 December: Two .30-cal holes – one in nosewheel door and one destroying tip tank light.
24 January 1966: One .30-cal hole in right side of boattail.
February: One .30-cal hole in left aileron.
8 March: One .30-cal hole in right tip tank.

These bullet holes suggest luck, skill, or high volumes of expended ammunition on the part of the enemy shooters. Other anecdotal reports from the war in Southeast Asia imply some gunners did not sufficiently lead their flying targets, resulting in misses or impacts noticeably on the aft portions of the airframes. Such is not the case with the majority of the Skoshi Tiger battle damage statistics.

The conclusion of Skoshi Tiger saw the equipment and personnel assigned to the 10th Fighter Commando Squadron (FCS), Third Tactical Fighter Wing, activated at Bien Hoa in the Republic of Vietnam on 8 March 1966. The 10th Fighter Commando Squadron served the

An ever-present HH-43 rescue helicopter motored in the distance near two Skoshi Tiger Freedom Fighters. Nearest F-5 carries napalm canisters; aircraft on the right is loaded with bombs. (AFHRA)

USAF in Vietnam until the squadron was deactivated on 17 April 1967. At that time, aircraft and equipment were transferred to the Vietnamese Air Force (VNAF).[72] Bob Titus commanded the 10th FCS. He flew one of seven additional F-5Cs brought to Vietnam in 1966 to bolster the unit's strength to 18 aircraft. Upon arrival at Bien Hoa, the refueling booms were removed from the new F-5s, Titus said, and all of the 10th FCS Freedom Fighters flew their missions without the booms. Missions for the 10th FCS did not include the likelihood of air-to-air engagements, so the F-5Cs were not flown with AIM-9 missiles on the wingtips, Titus recalled. The 10th FCS carried on the Skoshi Tiger tradition and name; some of the pilots even had tiger stripes painted on their flight helmets.[73]

Maintaining the Skoshi Tiger Freedom Fighters

Skoshi Tiger's maintenance chief is quoted as calling the F-5 the easiest and simplest aircraft to repair that he had encountered. Built low to the ground, access to most of the aircraft did not require maintenance stands. And when heavy tugs were needed to tow most Air Force fighters, three men could roll the F-5 on a hard surface. One

Air Force maintenance troops tended to the new Skoshi Tiger F-5s upon their arrival at Bien Hoa in October 1965. A replacement tire and wheel have been placed on the ramp and engine inlet screens installed as the job of keeping the Tigers flying unfolded. (AFHRA)

man could roll an F-5 J85 engine on a wheeled dolly. During the Skoshi Tiger deployment, on 6 February 1966, maintainers completed an engine change in one hour and 55 minutes, including the jet's test hop after the engine swap.[74]

Early Skoshi Tiger sorties were accompanied by problems with stores separation from the pylons, sometimes causing airframe damage. Contractor support helped fix this, and led to the squadron's F-5s being retrofitted with new pylons that improved the situation significantly, including the capability to jettison stores during an emergency. Nonetheless, it was thought prudent

to restrict the F-5s from carrying four BLU-1B napalm bombs due to the separation characteristics from the inboard pylons.[75]

Engine failures and engine changes received attention during Skoshi Tiger. At the end of the combat evaluation, squadron officials reported 77 engine removals and replacements. Fifty-nine of these were attributed to foreign object damage (FOD). No Skoshi J85 engines ever failed completely in flight, according to Air Force documents. FOD was frequently traced to debris from firing the nose-mounted 20-mm cannons. According to the official Skoshi Tiger history documentation: "In

This tent with sidewalls served the Skoshi Tiger chief of maintenance at Bien Hoa. (AFHRA)

late December 1965, officials decided to restrict firing the guns to emergency use or highly lucrative targets only, which drastically reduced foreign object damage during flight." The M-39 cannons in the Skoshi F-5 Freedom Fighters averaged about one malfunction for every 1,100 rounds of ammunition fired. By comparison, this was slightly better than the average for M-39 cannons used in F-100 Super Sabres.[76]

No other significant problem areas were noted with the Skoshi F-5s, although tire consumption was observed to be slightly higher than had been anticipated.

Skoshi Tiger Combat Evaluation Team

A 33-person combat evaluation team worked with the 4503rd Tactical Fighter Squadron (Provisional) to provide the basis for comparing the F-5 with other fighter types in the combat theater at that time. Comparisons were to include performance, weapons delivery accuracy, maintainability, reliability, maneuverability, survivability, and

vulnerability. Comparison data was initially furnished by the F-4 Phantom-equipped 47th Tactical Fighter Squadron at Ubon Air Base, Thailand, and after that unit rotated home, by the 12th Tactical Fighter Wing at Cam Ranh Bay, Vietnam. F-100 Super Sabres of the 307th Tactical Fighter Squadron at Bien Hoa provided data until rotating home in early December 1965; subsequent F-100 data came from three squadrons of the 3rd Tactical Fighter Wing. The F-104 Starfighter-equipped 435th Tactical Fighter Squadron at Da Nang was lined up for comparison but subsequently redeployed back to the U.S.

Objective and subjective data formed the core of the evaluation. "Team evaluators collected personal views of the pilots as well as those of forward air controllers in order to accurately measure the terminal effectiveness of the aircraft to deliver their ordnance on targets," the Air Force Skoshi Tiger history explained. Evaluation team members came to believe the observations of forward air controllers—FACs—were the best source of unbiased opinion on the terminal effec-

tiveness of the F-5 as well as the other comparison fighters. The statisticians were occasionally frustrated when changes in the availability of data necessitated urgent workarounds.[77]

When the data was reduced and analyzed, the final Skoshi Tiger report contained a warning about its conclusions: "Caution is recommended in taking action on, or quoting further, the conclusions contained herein without full consideration of all the possible qualifying factors contained in the body of the report."

With that caveat in mind, the report's conclusions included the following observations based exclusively on test data:[78] "Overall Evaluation: The F-5 weapon system was employed successfully in combat operations in Southeast Asia. It performed useful functions in all of the tactical air support roles in which it participated. Functional deficiencies associated with engine foreign-object damage and munition-release problems are such, however, that the F-5 aircraft as tested during Project Skoshi Tiger cannot be considered fully suitable for combat. With the correction of the above deficiencies, the F-5 may be considered as an adequate aircraft to complement, but not substitute for, the F-100 or F-4 in the total range of tactical air operations. The F-4 has inherent capabilities across the entire spectrum of tactical air roles far beyond that of both the F-5 and F-100."[79]

Overall reliability of the Skoshi Tiger F-5s was slightly better than that of the comparison F-100s, and "significantly better than the F-4," the report noted. Not counting periodic inspection man-hours, the trend in the tested aircraft also favored the Skoshi Tiger F-5s with a tally of 10.3 maintenance man-hours

per flying hour, versus 10.8 for the evaluated F-100s and 17.5 for the F-4s monitored. Under routine maintenance effort, turn-around times for the F-5 and F-100 were nearly the same, and both these fighters posted turn-around times 20 to 30 percent less than those of the evaluated F-4s. When accelerated maintenance effort was applied, F-100 turn-around times beat the F-5; no comparable data was received for the monitored F-4s. When quantifying specialist skills required for unscheduled maintenance, "the F-5 required slightly fewer man-hours than the F-100, and markedly fewer than the F-4," the Skoshi Tiger final evaluation noted.[80]

When it came to placing bombs on target, the Skoshi Tiger report did not have combat CEPs to compare. The report noted: "...sufficient comparative data on delivery effectiveness was obtained to reach the conclusion that there is no significant difference in the delivery accuracies of the three types of aircraft." Vulnerability data were not voluminous enough to enable the drawing of conclusions from the small sample of hit and loss incidents observed on all three types of aircraft studied. And logistical support of the three fighter types was not compared since supplies were furnished "by three totally different methods," the final report observed.[81]

The F-5 Skoshi Tiger evaluation team extrapolated some data to conclude that the practical combat radius of the F-5 carrying the equivalent of four M-117 bombs was about 120 to 150 nautical miles, as opposed to the pre-Skoshi Tiger computation of 230 nautical miles. Both the F-4 and F-100 could "carry heavier loads to greater distances than the F-5 on

Well over 300 bomb mission symbols and a friendly "zap" bulldog from a Marine attack squadron adorn the F-5 flown by Challen "Choni" Irvine in Vietnam. Irvine's helmet, resting atop the windscreen, has a visor that is appropriately tiger striped. Though the refueling boom has been removed from his F-5, part of its faired-in hardware remains visible on the fuselage beside the canopy. (Challen Irvine collection)

similar profiles and with identical times over the target. The greatest difference in capabilities exists at radii of about 150 NM (nautical miles) or less. At these distances, the F-4 has a payload potential of 2-1/2 times or greater than those of the other aircraft."[82]

It was a mixed bag—the big F-4 could clearly carry more ordnance, yet the final Skoshi report noted "...the F-5 and F-100 calculated sustained sortie rates are approximately the same, and from 20 to 30 percent greater than those of the F-4." On missions involving one refueling, the F-5 calculated ordnance delivery rate was considered comparable to that of the F-100 "out to about 220 NM, but would be less than the F-100 at greater distances." For unrefueled missions, the F-100 was calculated to have a better ordnance delivery rate than the F-5 "at radii beyond about 55 NM." F-5 capabilities "would be less than the F-4 at all radii," the report noted.[83]

Other statistical quirks were noted. While the F-5 pilots tended to have more total flight hours than the F-100 and F-4 pilots in the comparison, the F-5 pilots had fewer hours in their current fighter, the F-5, than the other fliers had in their current F-100s and F-4s. The report team did not infer a conclusion from this observation. The F-5s carried a 150-gallon centerline fuel tank on all but five bombing sorties. This configuration left four stores positions open for ordnance. The F-5s used 50-gallon wingtip fuel tanks on all sorties but the 32 logged combat-patrol and escort sorties, for which the wingtip tanks were replaced with one AIM-9B missile on each wingtip. The final Skoshi Tiger report indicates the practice of carrying (and firing) air-to-ground rockets on the inboard pylons was discontinued during the F-5 evaluation in an effort to reduce engine FOD. The F-5s typically carried four 750-lb M-117 bombs on inter-

Challen "Choni" Irvine paused on the boarding ladder of his F-5 with the crew chiefs who kept the Freedom Fighters flying at Bien Hoa in 1966. Close-to-the-ground stance of the diminutive F-5 is evident; this facilitated maintenance of the aircraft. (Challen Irvine collection)

Air Force pilots paused beside a later Vietnam-era F-5A, modified to become an F-5C (65-10525A) according to its data stenciling. (Craig Kaston collection)

diction sorties into Laos and North Vietnam. On the few unrefueled missions into these areas, only two M-117s were mounted to the small F-5s.[84]

Learning Curve

Preparing and deploying early F-5As for combat provided the Air Force with opportunities to expand the base of knowledge about the Freedom Fighter. The refueling probe, versions of which subsequently appeared on other F-5s, was first installed on Skoshi Tiger F-5 number 64-13314. Skoshi Tiger pilots helped evaluate the aircraft's air refueling system at Edwards AFB, California, in September 1965. The F-5A had no cockpit indicator to show external tank fuel quantity, diminishing the pilot's ability to know with certainty that his F-5 had received a full fuel transfer. "However," the Skoshi Tiger final report explained, "by noting the tanker off-load and by observing a slight siphoning or feathering of fuel from the external tanks as they become full, complete fuel transfers are reasonably confirmed."[85]

Aerial refueling in a Skoshi Tiger F-5 could be accomplished with the engines at military power settings at light gross weights. "As gross weight and/or altitude is increased, one or both afterburners are required," the Skoshi Tiger final report noted. "Because thrust increase from military power to maximum afterburner is almost linear, power response is excellent and afterburner power can be selected while hooked up if desired," the report continued. "The procedure adopted by the 4503 TAC Ftr Sq for the deployment was to stabilize eight to 10 feet behind the drogue, select minimum afterburner on one engine, and regulate thrust with the other engine in military power range. Power and flight-control response in the deployment configuration at 30,000 feet and 300 KIAS (knots indicated airspeed) is excellent." The F-5 fliers noticed during slow disconnects from the tanker drogue that a quantity of jet fuel estimated at several gallons would spew from the tanker hose,

apparently entering the F-5's left engine intake.

"There are no adverse effects from this and no indications in the cockpit either from engine instruments or fumes," the Skoshi Tiger final report said. F-5 pilots learned that the presence of the refueling boom on a Freedom Fighter caused different yaw angles linked to airspeed changes, requiring rudder trim inputs. F-5 and KC-135 refueling compatibility was deemed excellent.[86]

What the Pilots Said

Pilot interviews for the Skoshi Tiger F-5 fliers as well as inputs from F-4 and F-100 pilots taken for comparison indicate all of the questioned F-4 Phantom and 81 percent of the F-100 pilots believed their aircraft to be outstanding or at least satisfactory on takeoff roll. Sixty-four percent of the Skoshi Tiger F-5 pilots rated the F-5 at that time barely adequate or unsatisfactory.[87] Subsequent introduction of a nosewheel strut that could be hiked for better takeoff angle of attack did much to alleviate this issue in F-5 performance.

Northrop designers put some thought into cockpit layout and pilot visibility in the F-5, and this shows in Skoshi Tiger pilot ratings on visibility. Thirty-two percent of the Skoshi Tiger F-5 pilots interviewed said the F-5 has outstanding

One of the original Skoshi Tiger Freedom Fighters, 64-13315, was photographed in fresh camouflage paint in California before beginning its overseas journey into combat. (Northrop via Tony Chong collection)

visibility, the highest percentage for all three fighters compared. The remaining 68 percent of the F-5 pilots called the visibility adequate, again larger than either F-4 or F-100 pilots responding. The F-100 and F-4 each had a few respondents who rated the visibility unsatisfactory; no Skoshi Tiger pilots rated the F-5 that way. Subsequently, some Skoshi F-5 pilots may have had second thoughts as rain during slow flight and foreign object damage (FOD) during gunfire caused some Freedom Fighter windscreen issues.

Most F-5 pilots—58 percent—said their aircraft had satisfactory payload. Meanwhile, a whopping 65 percent of those who flew the big F-4 Phantom called its payload outstanding; only 5 percent of the F-5 pilots rated their aircraft that

way. More significantly, 32 percent of the F-5 pilots rated their aircraft's payload only barely adequate. Perhaps not surprisingly, after early incidents with pylon ejection problems, the highest rating the F-5 got for pylon ejection was a "barely adequate" from 21 percent of the Skoshi pilots interviewed; the majority of the F-5 fliers—79 percent—said pylon ejection was unsatisfactory. A later survey found the pylon issue had dropped to insignificance due to successful modification of the F-5 pylons.[88]

The heart of the matter—weapons delivery—brought some interesting diversity in observations by the interviewed fighter pilots. The percentage of pilots is reproduced in the table below, extracted from Appendix I, Annex B, of the

Weapons Delivery

	Outstanding			Satisfactory			Barely Adequate			Unsatisfactory		
	F-100	F-4	F-5	F-100	F-4	F-5	F-100	F-4	F-5	F-100	F-4	F-5
Strafe	64	44	78	35	50	22	1	6	0	0	0	0
Dive bomb	25	35	72	69	61	28	6	4	0	0	0	0
Rockets	30	45	38	65	51	33	3	4	14	2	0	14
Napalm	47	49	75	52	51	15	2	0	5	0	0	5
CBU	62	31	67	35	45	24	2	16	5	2	7	5

Ease of maintenance, including quick engine changes, impressed Skoshi Tiger maintainers. F-5 64-13316 was photographed during an engine change at Bien Hoa. (AFHRA)

Skoshi Tiger final report:

Missile findings are deleted from this excerpt since the report's writers said none of the aircraft types in the survey fired missiles in combat, making survey comments "misleading."[89]

Inadequacies in F-5 performance might be expected; after all, this was the first combat trial of an airplane not even built for the U.S. Air Force to take into battle. What is more remarkable is the fact that in four out of the five validated weapons delivery categories, 90 percent or more of the interviewed Skoshi Tiger F-5 pilots said the F-5 was at least satisfactory; many said it was outstanding.[90]

Where the diminutive F-5A/F-5C scored poorly was in the categories of range and loiter time. No Skoshi pilots called the F-5 outstanding in these areas, while a majority of F-5 pilots, 53 and 58 percent, respectively, found their Freedom Fighters to be barely ade-

quate in range and loiter time. Clear majorities of the F-4 and F-100 pilots rated their aircraft satisfactory in range and loiter time; there's probably no upper limit, save fatigue, to the amount of loiter time considered desirable when it comes to protecting friendly troops on the ground.[91]

The evaluators of Skoshi Tiger summed up many of their findings: "In comparative roles for the three aircraft, all three (pilot groups) agree that the least desirable roles are for escort of vehicles and helicopters. The F-100 was seen as ranking first or second in the role of CAS (close air support) or interdiction. The F-4 in CAP (combat air patrol) and the F-5 in CAS."[92]

Accuracy was summed with a reasonable caveat in the Skoshi evaluation report: "Where the FACs (forward air controllers) and the pilots were rating aspects which could be commonly observed, they were in general agreement in

ranking overall accuracy: F-100 first, F-5 second, and the F-4 third."[93]

While there was a high degree of positive feelings for the Skoshi Tiger F-5s by their operators, these fighter pilots were not without criticisms and suggestions on ways to make the F-5 better. Numerous suggestions to shorten the takeoff roll were filed, ranging from the extendable nosewheel strut to more power. Early in the Skoshi Tiger evaluation, missions were local. After going into Laos, where range became an issue, pilots criticized range and loiter time, and suggested greater internal fuel tankage and bigger external tanks—both of which subsequently came with the F-5E. Concern with compressor stalls, experienced sometimes during pullouts from weapons delivery passes, was voiced. This was especially worrisome on the few occasions when both engines experienced compressor stalls simultaneously, since the recovery sequence includes reducing power. Engine FOD was also a concern for the F-5 pilots in the Southeast Asia environment.[94]

Many of the recommendations proved prescient, as they were later adopted as the F-5 series evolved. At least four of the pilots suggested the addition of maneuvering flaps or slats, something the F-5E accommodated. Four pilots urged installation of a tailhook, also later adopted for emergency runway overruns. The suggestion of installing a computing gunsight was realized later too.

Something not done, even though suggested by 15 of the pilots, was the use of a "standard glass bulletproof windshield." Other jet fighters of the era typically used curved Plexiglas plastic panels in the windscreen on either side of a flat glass center windscreen that might

be laminated or made of layers with air space for defogging, whether or not it was actually "bulletproof." The F-5 used a curved wraparound plastic one-piece windscreen instead. This came in for criticism during Skoshi Tiger, the final report noted, because "debris from the guns pits the windshield and causes FOD to the engine." The report captured the pilots' reasoning: "...a glass windshield would be less susceptible to pitting by the debris from the guns."[95] Years later, Skoshi Tiger and 10th Fighter Commando Squadron F-5 pilot Bob Titus elaborated on the FOD problem: "We had a lot of engine damage due to the fragmentation cloud produced when strafing. The exceptional close tolerances of the small compressor blades didn't like that, so we were forced to increase slant range for pullout."[96]

Eleven comments urged improvement in F-5 cockpit air conditioning, rain removal, and defogging systems. "Continuous operation in a poor weather environment brought out a need to improve the air conditioning system," the report noted.[97] John Lisella, who flew F-5s in Southeast Asia combat, recalled how the lack of a rain removal system caused perils: "No rain removal system – tough to land in a rain storm...."[98] His comment was echoed by Bob Titus: "Yes, if in formation you went through a rain shower you were suddenly in a fish bowl! Northrop subsequently came up with (a) spray can of wetting agent which could be activated from the cockpit and which improved forward visibility for landing in the rain."[99] (Raindrops were less likely to pose a vision hazard at higher speeds where they would be whipped away in the slipstream.)

Releasing bombs in a dive, a Skoshi Tiger F-5 flew into battle in Southeast Asia, racking up statistics that validated the Freedom Fighter's combat worthiness while pointing out some areas that could be improved with later models. (Tony Chong collection)

In Their Own Words

A number of early USAF F-5 Southeast Asia combat pilots have offered comments on the little Northrop jet they flew. Bob Titus, who went on to command the follow-on squadron to Skoshi Tiger, the 10th Fighter Commando Squadron, in Vietnam, discussed the F-5 as a weapons delivery system: "The IPs (instructor pilots) at Willy (Williams AFB, Arizona, the F-5 training base), consistently won gunnery meets over F-100s from Luke and Nellis with wide margins. On my first bombing mission from Willy to the Gila Bend range, I got two hits on low angle (skip bombing)... and... dive bombing. My IP, Dick Lougie, beat me as he got two shacks on (a) dive. It was a solid platform with excellent lateral response to which I attribute the results."[100]

Titus recalled: "In combat we were usually the FAC's dive bomber of choice." He added: "We could carry four external stores, but we only had two 20-mm cannons. Some critics pointed out that we had limited range, but I remember responding, 'What the hell, we're bombing as far off the end of the runway as the B-52s, and they're coming all the way from Guam.'"[101]

Bill Rippy, who served as Bob Titus' operations officer, acknowledged the limited range of the early combat F-5s, but he had praise for the Freedom Fighter, saying it "was a good formation aircraft and had excellent maneuverability—I'm sure that's why it was selected as the aggressor aircraft to simulate the Russian fighters out at Nellis." Perhaps Rippy said it best: "Of all the fighters I flew, I would say that the F-5 was the 'sportscar' fighter."[102]

A lot of geography has passed under the wings of F-5s since U.S. Air Force pilots first took the Freedom Fighter into battle in 1965. Just as the warplanes of World War II required upgrades dictated by combat experience, so did the F-5 improve over time.

THE T-38 TALON

If the U.S. Air Force developed only scant interest in the F-5 for its own use, the sleekly similar T-38 Talon was an unqualified success in Air Force service. With its supersonic speed, slightly elevated rear seat for the instructor pilot, wide-track landing gear, and afterburner-equipped engines, the sporty T-38 proved to be the right steppingstone for student pilots who had already mastered the slow, straight-wing T-37.

Spanning more than four decades of flight, the T-38 has trained generations of Air Force pilots. Along the way, it has seen service as an aggressor aircraft in dissimilar aircraft combat training, and it has been the steed of NASA

Northrop's amazing blend of art and science shows up in photos like this banking shot of a clean T-38A Talon, revealing the sculpting that coaxed optimal performance from the jet. (AFFTC/HO collection)

Not all T-38s remained pristine white; some received variegated camouflage schemes like this blue and gray speedster, serial 61-851, from Randolph Air Force Base, photographed in 1997.

astronauts. The U.S. Navy has operated a few T-38s as aggressors, and the U.S. Air Force Thunderbirds demonstration team switched from F-4E Phantoms to T-38s in 1974. Talons have also been used to train foreign pilots. As of this writing, a scant few T-38s have made their way into the civilian market (as have some foreign F-5s).

The product of Northrop's quest in the 1950s for capable, yet relatively inexpensive, high-performance jet aircraft, the Talon originated in company efforts as the N-156T, a clear derivative of N-156 fighter studies then underway. Northrop's studies complemented the Air Force's forecast need for a supersonic trainer that more closely matched the traits of front-line fighter aircraft many Air Force pilots would subsequently fly. Before the advent of the T-38, undergraduate pilot training (UPT) in the Air Force included stick time in the venerable Lockheed T-33 Shooting Star, itself a derivative of the 1944 P-80 jet fighter. As the performance gulf widened between the durable old T-33 and the jet fighters then coming into service, the time was right for an all-new training aircraft.

The Air Force bundled its expectations for a new jet trainer under the nomenclature TZ. Northrop courted the Air Force with its N-156T design, and on 15 June 1956, the Air Force authorized development of a pair of prototypes plus a static test airframe. A full-scale mock-up of the so-called

Front cockpit of a well-worn T-38 at the Air Force Flight Test Center (AFFTC) was photographed on 5 January 1976. Armament switches suggest this aircraft was configured for lead-in fighter training. (AFFTC/HO collection)

Blue camouflaged T-38A 65-10341 from Holloman AFB, New Mexico, carried a travel pod on the centerline station on a cross-country trip during which it stopped at McChord AFB, Washington, in June 1984.

Head-on view of a T-38A shows stand-off inlets far enough from the fuselage surface to avoid boundary layer air turbulence. "Coke bottle" area-rule phenomenon is clearly visible in narrowing of fuselage at wing junction. (AFFTC/HO collection)

AT-38A 60-576, carrying a practice bomb dispenser, leads two other Talons during AT-38 lead-in fighter evaluation in January 1976. (AFFTC/HO collection)

Northrop TZ-156 featured a swept vertical tail that soon changed into the characteristic double tapered shape of the T-38 and F-5 series. Wind tunnel testing refined some aspects of the new trainer, and by the time the first YT-38 was trucked from Northrop's plant in Hawthorne, California, to Edwards Air Force Base for flight testing in early 1959, it was in many respects a matured design. So competent was its execution that the T-38 did not require any aerodynamic changes during flight testing—a difficult mark to achieve with a supersonic design of that era.[103]

Northrop's Lew Nelson made the T-38's first flight from Edwards

Air Force Base on 10 April 1959. Four days and two flights later, Nelson nudged the YT-38 through the sound barrier, and the first purpose-built supersonic trainer made good one of its fundamental promises. The test program went well. For initial testing with a single pilot, the convenience of a rear cockpit for carrying test instrumentation was sometimes visible, as the rear canopy occasionally was painted white as a sun shield. Six months into the T-38 test program at Edwards AFB, in October 1959 the Air Force gave Northrop a letter contract for 50 more Talons. An additional 144 T-38s were ordered by the Air Force in 1960, and in 1961 the production rate was set at 12 Talons a month. Total production

NASA T-38 landing gear retracts quickly after leaving the runway in this photo taken in 2000. Northrop devised an aerodynamic solution to boost the retraction speed of the main landing gear to ensure the gear was fully retracted before the accelerating jet exceeded its maximum gear-down speed.

T-38 rear cockpit view taken in November 1975 at the Air Force Flight Test Center at Edwards AFB shows placement of rearview mirrors on canopy frame. Reflection in left mirror may indicate this is aircraft 63-8135, a T-38A-50-NO. T-38s have been used for many flight tests, chase duties, and USAF Test Pilot School programs.

Like the early N-156 fighter design, the T-38 went through swept-tail mock-up iteration before the F-5/T-38 series arrived at its final shared tail shape. (Northrop via Craig Kaston collection)

A pair of white USAF T-38s on a cross-country flight paused at McChord Air Force Base in September 1986.

The U.S. Air Force's Thunderbirds demonstration team flew T-38s from 1974 into the early 1980s. Thunderbird pilots flew their T-38s solo from the front cockpit as seen in the photo.

run for the T-38A was 1,189 aircraft.

Some 2,000 test-flights later, the T-38 flight test program was completed in February 1961. When released to the USAF Air Training Command, the T-38 quickly proved its merit in operational surroundings. Early in 1962, Air Force test pilot Maj. Walter Daniel used a T-38 to set four international time-to-climb records, including a rush to 39,372 feet in 95.74 seconds.[104]

T-38 Powerplant

General Electric's J85 turbojet engine, central to Northrop's early success with the T-38 and F-5 series, was still maturing when the first airframes were ready to test. The first two Talons flew in the beginning of the test program with YJ85-GE-1 versions of the engines that were not fitted with afterburners. Other YT-38s in the flight test program used YJ85-GE-5 engines with afterburners, and rated at 3,600 lbs static thrust. Production Talons fly with a pair of J85-GE-5 engines rated at 3,850 lbs static thrust.[105]

It can be argued that the somewhat modest thrust levels of early T-38 powerplants added emphasis to the Northrop quest for airframe aerodynamic efficiency, resulting in some of the T-38's and F-5's most aesthetic traits.

As part of Northrop's overarching quest for simplicity, engine mounts in the T-38 consisted of overhead tracks with two-point mounts. Access was enhanced by the removal of the angled lower aft fuselage structure. Each engine, including its afterburner, weighs about 525 lbs. The electrical and hydraulic accessory systems are powered by a drive shaft at the front of each engine. The engines can be disconnected and removed from the

Thunderbird T-38 maintainers raised the hinged windscreen on one of the team's Talons to perform work before an air show, circa 1974.

airframe without affecting these accessory systems. Low-pressure air from a mobile ground power cart is used to start the T-38 engines.[106]

Fuel totaling 600 gallons is carried in bladder tanks installed behind the cockpits in the T-38's fuselage. The tanks can be filled via gravity filler caps atop the fuselage or by using a single-point refueling fitting mounted ventrally, which can service all tanks simultaneously.

T-38's Unique Wing

Even Northrop's cost-conscious design gurus knew the T-38A's training mission differed enough from the F-5's combat role to warrant some significant tailoring of each airframe. While F-5s incorporated leading-edge maneuvering flaps and an angular extension from the wing to the fuselage in the inlet area, the T-38 shunned these devices as unnecessary to its basic training duties, although the wings of both aircraft are of essentially the same planform.

Like the F-5, the T-38A uses a single-piece wing. On the Talon,

Carrying the unusual mission designation "AT-38 LEAD-IN FIGHTER" on the inlet, AT-38 (60-0576) tested the use of a centerline-mounted SUU-11 20-mm gun pod at Edwards AFB when photographed in January 1976. (AFFTC/HO collection)

minus hardware for tip tanks, the wing spans 25 feet, 4 inches. Trailing edge plain flaps drop next to the fuselage to increase drag and lift for low-speed flight.

Flight Controls

Flight controls in the T-38 are hydraulically operated. To give the student and instructor pilot a sense of "feel" of control forces comparable to manually controlled aircraft, Northrop created artificial feel with a system of springs and weights. Hydraulic stability augmentation for the rudder and all-flying horizontal tail helps damp out pitch and yaw oscillations.

In 1966 West Germany (Federal Republic of Germany) opted to conduct its Luftwaffe student pilot

Two test program T-38A Talons flew over outlying parts of the Air Force Flight Test Center (AFFTC) complex near Rogers Dry Lake at Edwards Air Force Base, California, early in the evaluation of the aircraft. Talon nearest to camera (58-1191) is the first of two YT-38A prototypes built. Covered rear canopy provides sunscreen for test instrumentation. (AFFTC/HO collection)

training over the vastness of Texas, at Sheppard AFB. For this, Germany bought 46 Talons for use in the United States, carrying U.S. Air Force markings. Subsequently, pilots from other NATO nations would use T-38s at Sheppard as part of the Euro-NATO Joint Jet Pilot Training Program.

The U.S. Navy became a user of T-38s starting in 1969, with five Talons assigned initially to that service's test pilot school at Patuxent River, Maryland. The last of the line of Talons was delivered to the U.S. Air Force on 31 January 1972 at Northrop's Palmdale, California, facility.

B-Model Talon

Some A-model Talons were modified as AT-38Bs with provision for a practice bomb dispenser and gunsight. These aircraft provide additional specialized

The number one YT-38 was photographed in April 1959, when Air Force aircraft still used buzz numbers on the sides of the fuselage. Letters TF were assigned to the T-38; 191 is the last three numbers of this aircraft's serial number. (AFFTC/HO collection)

A convergence of legends and legends-to-be occurred when celebrated aviation artist Jack Leynnwood painted a pair of T-38s in presumed silver finish over the heart of Randolph Air Force Base in San Antonio, where so many Air Force fliers have been trained. (Northrop via Craig Kaston collection)

Painted blue overall, this civilian-operated T-38, registered N38TG, was a visitor to the 2000 Experimental Aircraft Association AirVenture show in Oshkosh, Wisconsin. It was said to be constructed from a wing, a fuselage, and thousands of spare parts purchased from multiple sources, including a pair of low-time J85 engines from Norway.

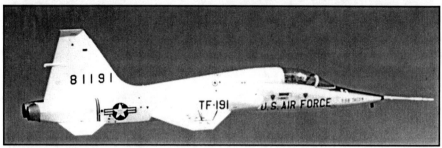

training to prepare combat pilots for the sophisticated fighters and bombers they will fly operationally.

T-38C

The USAF Air Education and Training Command took delivery of the first improved T-38C in 2001. Another modification of existing T-38As, the T-38C brings the Talon up to date with 21st century improvements including a glass integrated avionics cockpit display. The C-model also incorporates a propulsion modernization program in which the entire inlet and fuselage structure aft of the inlet back to fuselage station 325 have been redesigned to increase thrust available at takeoff. Other C-model upgrades include replacement of some engine components. The Air Force forecasts using the renewed T-38Cs at least until 2020.[107]

Meanwhile, since 2001 Northrop has been building and delivering to the Air Force 55 replacement wings for T-38s to keep the fleet viable until the advent of a new Talon wing design, forecast to enter production in 2006 for retrofitting the entire remaining fleet of about 500 T-38s.[108]

The first YT-38, photographed in May 1960, showed placement of turbine warning stripes on aft fuselage. Jet aircraft frequently used red stripes to indicate the plane in which whirling turbine blades could be hazardous if accidentally shed from the engine core. (AFFTC/HO collection)

Northrop commissioned artist Jack Leynnwood, known for his compelling model box art renderings, to paint early swept-tail T-38 concepts in flight, accented by a heroic jet pilot figure in the foreground. (Northrop via Craig Kaston collection)

Talons for the Astronaut Corps

When NASA wanted aircraft in which astronauts could maintain their high-performance piloting skills, the agency chose the T-38 in 1964. By 2004, NASA counted 32 T-38s at the agency's airfield facilities adjacent to the Johnson Space Center in Houston, Texas. More than 100 astronauts in NASA at that time used the Talons for flying proficiency and training. Proving the Northrop team's life cost vision of

Thunderbird crews performed cockpit mount-up in unison at the beginning of a flight demonstration at Paine Field, Washington, circa 1974.

A few T-38 carcasses were scavenged at Davis-Monthan AFB, Arizona, to keep other Talons flying. Unusual are two all-gray paint schemes; fuselage nearest camera carries tail number 10862 in this July 1982 photo.

Many aircraft operators celebrated the American bicentennial in 1976 with the application of patriotic red-white-and-blue special paint schemes. This U.S. Navy T-38 flown at the China Lake weapons test facility in California's Mojave Desert featured a dazzling red-and-white sunburst pattern on the wings, a red-and-white nose and upper fuselage, dark blue lower fuselage and horizontal tail surfaces decorated with white stars, and an absence of national insignia. (U.S. Navy)

A T-38 in pieces at the Air Force's Aircraft Maintenance and Regeneration Center (AMARC) in Tucson, Arizona, on 22 February 2005 looked like a giant model kit awaiting assembly. White plastic Spraylat protective coating draped low over the front cockpit is evidence that the front canopy and windscreen have been removed from this Talon.

Rows of T-38s on wooden stands surrender parts to keep the rest of the Talon fleet flying. Photo taken 22 February 2005.

the 1950s to be correct, NASA is said to have considered replacing its T-38s with F-16s or F/A-18s in the late 1980s, but ultimately rejected the newer fighters as too expensive to operate in this role.[109]

Most of the Houston T-38s have been upgraded to N-model status in the years since 2000, and are expected to serve NASA into 2040. NASA's T-38Ns have replaced the Northrop ejection seat with a new Martin Baker ejection seat that increases the ejection envelope significantly, to include zero speed, zero altitude, on up to a speed of 600 knots. Previous T-38 seats required the aircraft to be moving at least 55 knots, and were restricted in use to no more than 550 knots at time of ejection. NASA's T-38 seat upgrade prompted interest from the Air Force for its own fleet of Talons.[110]

NASA T-38s at Johnson Space Center have also received wider engine inlets to facilitate NASA's largely subsonic mission profiles. The new design barely crimped top speed from Mach 1.17 to Mach 1.16.[111] Significantly, the new inlet allows NASA T-38s to take off from higher-altitude fields at hotter ambient temperatures than previously, by increasing the safety margin in the event of the loss of one engine during critical phases of takeoff. The wider inlets give the T-38 nearly 30 percent better climb performance, and make

Strategically placed wooden stands enabled workers to salvage needed landing gear struts from T-38s in storage in Arizona to keep other Talons airworthy.

Stripped of paint, yet protected with white plastic Spraylat material, a T-38 clearly shows angled rivet pattern on vertical fin. Photo taken at AMARC, Tucson, Arizona, 22 February 2005.

low-speed operations more efficient.[112]

General Electric improved on its legendary J85 engine in the NASA T-38s by devising exhaust duct ejectors that contribute to improved hot-weather, high-field-elevation performance. This feature is also said to deliver 8 to 10 percent improved fuel efficiency at cruise speed.

Cockpits of NASA T-38s undergo upgrades, too. Cathode ray tube (CRT) displays have replaced some traditional round "steam gauge" dials in the NASA Talons, and global positioning system (GPS) equipment is on board.

LATE DEVELOPMENTS

The F-5A's demonstrated premise of simplicity in an air-to-ground jet fighter ensured its longevity. But a proliferation of capable MiG-21s in the air forces of Soviet- and Chinese-supported countries argued for the creation of a better air-to-air capability for America's allies who faced this potential MiG threat. Even before the U.S. Air Force formally identified the need for a new-generation Military Assistance Program jet fighter to meet the MiGs, Northrop began assimilating a host of improvements from international F-5A contracts, while grooming an improved J85 turbojet with General Electric.

Showing the capacity for ever-more firepower, F-5E 71-1418 (the number two E-model) evaluated a centerline 30-mm gun pod when photographed 5 March 1979. Motion picture cameras mounted on the wing pylons were trained on the gun pod. (AFFTC/HO collection)

J85 Revisited

The sporty little J85 engine that helped Northrop realize the promise of the original N-156 project became even more capable in the late 1960s under continued development by General Electric. This ultimately contributed to the increased performance of the F-5E and F-models. In tests the J85-21 turbojet indicated almost 23 percent more thrust than the earlier F-5s' J85-13 powerplants.

By the summer of 1969, General Electric was flight testing a pair of J85-21s in a modified F-5B at the GE contractor site on Edwards AFB. The evolving concept for a souped-up Freedom Fighter aircraft was called the F-5-21.

In addition to its markedly higher thrust, the J85-21 engine under test actually showed small decreases in fuel consumption in some flight regimes. The -21 grew in weight by less than 100 lbs, topping out at 670 lbs in the test phase. Substituting titanium for

In January 1974, F-5E number 01386 was evaluated carrying BLU-27 ordnance under the wings. (AFFTC/HO collection)

steel in compressor construction minimized weight increase. The J85-21 improved on the thrust-to-weight ratio of its J85 predecessors, posting a ratio of 7.5:1 compared with 6.8:1 for the earlier J85-13. To get the extra power, GE added another stage to the front of the J85's previous eight-stage compressor, along with other compressor modifications. The J85-21 grew in length by about 7 inches as a result of the new compressor stage. Maximum diameter across the compressor remained 21 inches for both models of the J85. To take advantage of the -21's increased capabilities, GE engineers redesigned F-5 inlets to promote greater airflow.[113]

The F-5B-21 demonstrator incorporated plenum chamber takeoff doors to allow more engine air intake during takeoff. Other refinements, including a two-position nosegear that had been a customer request on some earlier F-5s, were incorporated in the F-5B-21. As early as January 1969, the Air Force issued a contract change notice to Northrop to substitute the -21 engines on F-5As scheduled for delivery in late 1970.[114]

Northrop Stays in the Saddle

Around the time of the F-5B-21 flight test, the Air Force decided in the fall of 1969 to hold a competition to select a new International Fighter Aircraft. Northrop's F-5-21 competed against proposals from McDonnell Douglas, LTV, and Lockheed. On 20 November 1970, the F-5-21 was announced the winner. (The name International Fighter is used in some Air Force news releases about the F-5E, with the name Tiger II included parenthetically; Tiger II is the generally accepted name for the F-5E and F-series.)

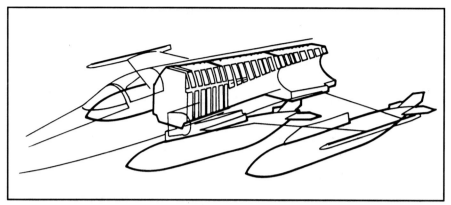

Bold lines indicate internal and external fuel tankage available to the F-5E in this Northrop line drawing. Fuselage space between the inlets and between the engines carried jet fuel. (Northrop via Craig Kaston collection)

Part of a fighter's flight test program includes flutter tests with various external stores configurations, as seen on an F-5E in the test program at Edwards AFB in December 1975. (AFFTC/HO collection)

Test F-5E was photographed carrying four smart bombs from wing pylons. Pylon nearest camera is stenciled "FLIGHT TEST PYLON." (Northrop via Craig Kaston collection)

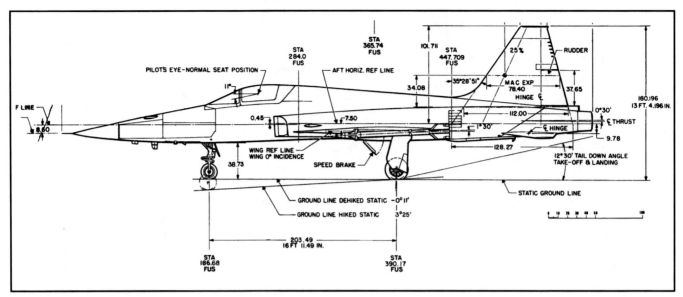

Detailed F-5E side elevation line art shows two ground plane references representing the nose gear in taxiing and hiked takeoff positions. (Northrop via Craig Kaston collection)

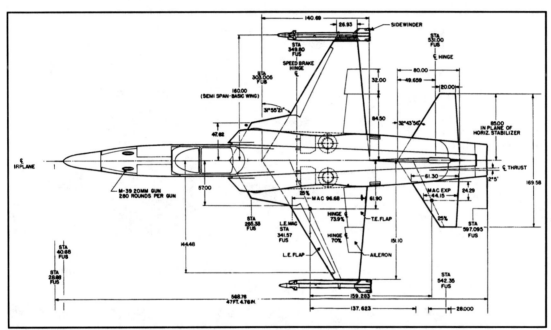

Dimensioned top view of an F-5E shows placement of ventral speed brakes and location of retracted main-wheels. Upper fuselage above wing has more noticeable area-rule curvature than dotted line representing lower fuselage edges beneath wing. (Northrop via Craig Kaston collection)

Northrop received a fixed-price incentive contract for engineering development and production of the new model F-5 on 8 December 1970.[15] A 1975 Air Force fact sheet described the F-5E's mission "primarily as an air superiority fighter for local air defense with a secondary air-to-ground capability."

Northrop's F-5 team groomed their aircraft to include many new features. Subtly, yet importantly, the new F-5's fuselage was widened and lengthened to accommodate the new longer engines and the wider inlets they required, as well as to maintain supersonic drag parameters. Wing area increased; a bigger tapered leading edge extension (LEX) was installed from the leading edge of the wings near the root to the fuselage. As part of the increased sophistication required in the 1970s to combat anticipated foes, the F-5-21 was fitted with an integrated fire-control radar system with a lead computing gunsight.[16]

In January 1971, the Air Force changed the new super F-5's nomenclature from F-5-21 to F-5E. Subsequently, it gained the name Tiger II, an oblique homage to the F-5As of the Air Force's Skoshi Tiger combat evaluation in Vietnam.

With a goal of improving air combat maneuvering, Northrop made specific changes to the F-5 airframe to create the E-model. The enlarged leading-edge extension (LEX) at the wing root of the F-5E is

Continued on page 71

THE NORTHROP F-5/F-20/T-38 IN COLOR

Imaginative camouflage schemes are a hallmark of F-5 aggressor aircraft like this E-model equipped with radar warning receivers (RWR), and photographed at NAS Fallon on 12 October 2005.

Tiger stripes for a Tiger II; this F-5E (160795) of Navy squadron VFC-13 at Fallon, Nevada, in October 2005 has all markings painted in the same subdued tan as the tiger stripes.

Perhaps an homage to the black F-5 "bad guy MiGs" from the movie Top Gun, this gloss black F-5E of Navy squadron VFC-13, photographed 12 October 2005, is an air show favorite. Large individual aircraft numbers (25) mimicked the style of some potentially hostile air forces when adopted a number of years ago for the American F-5 combat training fleet.

Two grays and a blue mimic sky and cloud hues on an aggressor F-5E of squadron VFC-13 at Fallon, Nevada, in October 2005.

F-5B with tip tanks and quasi-Southeast Asia camouflage begins a training sortie at Williams Air Force Base, Arizona, in January 1980.

Blue and gray camouflage breaks up the lines of a Royal Thai Air Force F-5E parked at Clark Air Base in the Philippines in January 1983.

Right: Brandishing dummy napalm bomb tanks during an evaluation, F-5A-15-NO (63-8370) banked over Lake Isabella in the mountains not far from Edwards AFB on 29 June 1964. This aircraft may subsequently have been renumbered and remanufactured to F-5B two-seater configuration. (AFFTC/HO collection)

Silver USAF F-5E aggressor (tail number 01388) used large centerline fuel tank for overwater flights to or from Kadena Air Base, Okinawa, when photographed in October 1985. Auxiliary engine air doors are open on the fuselage aft of insignia.

Tiger-tailed silver F-5F number 889 topped clouds over California on 25 September 1974. (AFFTC/HO collection)

By January 1980, former test aircraft F-5F 889 was a camouflaged USAF instructional aircraft with two tigers on its tail at Williams AFB, Arizona.

WARBIRDTECH
SERIES

Before the Navy applied red stars to the tails of its F-5 Top Gun aggressors, they carried a small squadron badge on the vertical fin representing a MiG-like aircraft in the gunsight reticle. Photo taken in January 1980 at the Top Gun school at NAS Miramar, California.

Carrying an air-to-surface missile shape on the centerline, F-20 N4416T employed a two-tone gray camouflage scheme at the time of this photograph. The small F-20 test and demonstration fleet underwent several paint changes. (AFFTC/HO collection)

F-20 Tigershark number 82-0062 flew in a dazzling red-and-white company paint scheme for this photo over the Edwards AFB flight line. (AFFTC/HO collection)

Gray Tiger F-5E of VFC-13 at Fallon, Nevada, was ready for a training sortie against inbound aircraft on 12 October 2005.

His helmet visor emblazoned with a red star, a USAF aggressor F-5E pilot taxied over taxiway stripes at Kadena Air Base, Okinawa, in May 1984.

Aging color photo depicts early version of the Northrop N-156F fighter proposal with traditional ribbed windscreen, swept tail, and fillets at aft wing/fuselage junction—features not carried into final configuration. (Northrop via Tony Chong collection)

Canadian A-model Freedom Fighter photographed at Abbotsford, British Columbia, in August 1976 featured European-style camouflage; Canadian CF-5s were used to bolster NATO forces.

Canadian aggressor CF-5A with refueling receptacle attached to right side of fuselage landed after an airshow performance in July 1984.

Wearing ceremonial red-and-white colors, this Canadian CF-5A of 419 Squadron attended the Abbotsford International Air Show in British Columbia in August of 1989.

A stylized air superiority camouflage scheme was applied to some USAF T-38s like this one taxiing at the Experimental Aircraft Association AirVenture 2000 show in Oshkosh, Wisconsin.

WARBIRDTECH
SERIES

Northrop adorned a pair of Freedom Fighters in Canadian markings in the 1960s when that country was considering buying the F-5. Interesting tail designators (CT-5 on F-5B in foreground and CF-5 on A-model behind it) gave way to a number of different nomenclatures for Freedom Fighters in Canadian service. (Craig Kaston collection)

With his tiger-striped helmet resting on the windscreen of his USAF F-5C, Skoshi Tiger (10th Fighter Commando Squadron) pilot Challen "Choni" Irvine smiled for the camera in 1966 in Bien Hoa, Republic of Vietnam. The aircraft is a 63-model, marked as an F-5C beside the cockpit. Protrusion on fuselage below helmet is a vestige of the removable refueling receptacle used by the C-models to fly across the Pacific. (Challen Irvine collection)

Navy Talon 1594 at the weapons test facility at China Lake, California, in January 1978 may be one of four DT-38 drone director aircraft.

The drama of night operations in a sleek T-38 Talon was immortalized by aviation artist Jack Leynnwood for Northrop. (Northrop via Craig Kaston collection)

A crisp echelon of four early Talons from the first production batch used high-visibility orange markings and fuselage buzz numbers when photographed in the vicinity of Edwards AFB on 28 December 1960. More than four decades later, T-38s were still a mainstay in USAF pilot training. (AFFTC/HO collection)

Brilliant orange Navy T-38 served test programs at China Lake when photographed on a crisp winter desert day in January 1978.

Splinter camouflage was used on this U.S. Navy T-38 getting a second career at China Lake in January 1978. F-86 Sabres behind the Talon were used as drone targets for years over China Lake's desert test ranges.

Winter rains have washed life into the grasses beneath thousands of stored aircraft at the joint-services Aircraft Maintenance and Regeneration Center (AMARC) in Tucson, Arizona. A T-38 in the foreground, its forward fuselage supported by a brace to allow its nose gear to be salvaged for another Talon, is backed by a wilderness of surplus F-4 Phantoms and T-tailed C-141 Starlifters in the distance as the morning sun pierces cloud cover. Photo taken 22 February 2005.

With South Vietnamese air force markings on the tail, this Freedom Fighter (65-10544) was photographed at base with incredible battle damage to the right J85 engine. (Tony Chong collection)

A couple years after the American bicentennial, this spectacular T-38, number 1596, supported test programs at the Navy's China Lake weapons test area near Ridgecrest in California's Mojave Desert.

Continued from page 64

2.75 times as big as that on the F-5A, to increase lift at high angles of attack during fighter maneuvers. A side benefit of the redesigned LEX is enhanced lift during takeoff and landing. The optimized LEX on the F-5E can also produce drag at high angles of attack, a phenomenon that a skilled pilot might use as a last-ditch maneuver to force an attacker to overshoot the F-5, although some fighter pilots do not endorse bleeding off energy like that.

The greater fuselage volume allowed internal fuel stowage to increase from the F-5A's 3,790 lbs to 4,360 lbs in the E-model. The F-5E also features a centerline stores pylon farther aft than on the A-model. This serves dual purposes: It permits carrying the long 275-gallon fuel tank while still clearing the nosewheel, and it moves the center of gravity slightly aft when carrying a heavy store on the pylon, which can reduce the takeoff roll.

Underwing fuel tanks can also be carried. The ability to carry substantially more fuel than the F-5A (which had a centerline tank capacity of only 150 gallons, as well as smaller internal fuel tanks) gives the F-5E greater mission radius plus a ferry range of more than 1,540

An F-model is connected to the refueling hose of a Marine Corps KC-130 tanker in this March 1977 photo. (AFFTC/HO collection)

statute miles (1,340 nautical miles) without dropping the external tanks. The F-5E is said to have a combat air patrol mission radius of 570 nautical miles.[17]

The widening of the fuselage on the F-5E permits the ventral speed brakes to be spaced farther

outboard from the centerline; with diagonal cutouts strategically placed, the speed brakes can clear larger centerline stores. Speed brake extension without a centerline store is 45 degrees, curtailed to 30 degrees with a centerline store. An interconnect between the speed

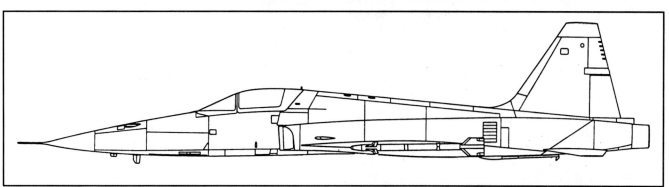

Left-side elevation drawing of the F-5E shows placement of auxiliary engine louver doors on fuselage side near base of vertical fin. (Northrop via Craig Kaston collection)

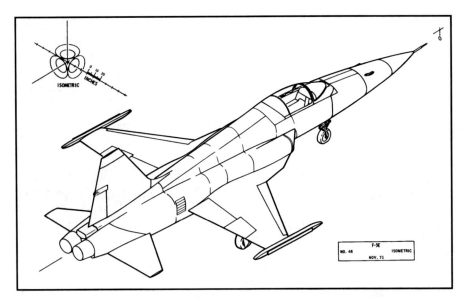

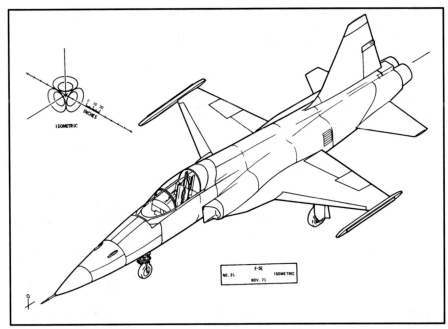

At once simple and exacting, these elegant Northrop isometric drawings of the F-5E reveal salient traits of the single-seat Tiger II design. (Northrop via Craig Kaston collection)

Removal of the nose reveals bulkhead details on a U.S. Navy Top Gun F-5E at Miramar Naval Air Station in January 1980.

brake and the all-flying horizontal tail minimizes the need for trim changes during speed brake extension and retraction. (Speed brakes and wing flaps interconnected with the horizontal tail trim are also featured on the F-5A and F-5B.)

The F-5E standardized other devices which had shown up on some, but not all, customer F-5As, including auxiliary air inlet doors to aid the engines during takeoff and slow flight, and a two-position nosegear strut to accommodate taxiing visibility as well as improved (shortened) takeoff roll. The strut could be lengthened 11.5 inches for takeoff, giving the F-5E a three-degree nose-up attitude that improves horizontal stabilator performance for rotation and shortens takeoff distance.

While a full-up armed and loaded F-5E could weigh a ton more than a similarly outfitted F-5A, the thrust-to-weight ratio for takeoff in the E-model is 57 percent compared with only 45 percent in the older A-model. As an air superiority fighter, the F-5E did not require tip tanks common to the F-5A, but comes with air-to-air missile rails standard on the wingtips. No doubt of comfort to the pilots who sweated out rain squalls in Skoshi Tiger F-5s in Vietnam, the E-model promised a rain-removal system as standard.

The F-5E has a wing area more than 9 percent greater than that of the F-5A, with 186 square feet versus 170 square feet. The increase is primarily due to the wider fuselage, which effectively extends the wings outboard 8-1/2 inches from the fuselage centerline. This helps keep the E-model's wing loading only 4 lbs per square foot higher than that of an F-5A. A-model wing loading is 68 lbs per square foot; E-model

wing loading is 71 lbs per square foot (at 50 percent fuel weight and 30,000 feet altitude). Keeping wing loading low is one way to enable maneuverability in a fighter; the World War II Grumman F6F Hellcat, said to have the largest wing area of any contemporary fighter, enjoyed good maneuverability as a result. The larger LEX and the use of maneuvering flaps increase the F-5E's lift in high-G conditions (turning or pitching maneuvers). This works to the advantage of the F-5E in a turning dogfight.

F-5Es and Fs have either a maneuver flap system or an auto flap system. Aircraft identified as E, E-1, E-2, F, or F-1 have the maneuver flap system; E-3 and F-2 aircraft

use the auto flap system. The interconnected leading and trailing edge flaps optimize the wing for all aspects of flight from takeoff

through cruise and maneuvering, to landing. The wing flaps are mechanically interconnected with the horizontal tail to minimize the need for

Packing only a pair of wingtip-mounted AIM-9 air-to-air missiles, a silver-painted F-5E banked near the Sierra Nevada Mountains of California during the Tiger II test program. (AFFTC/HO collection)

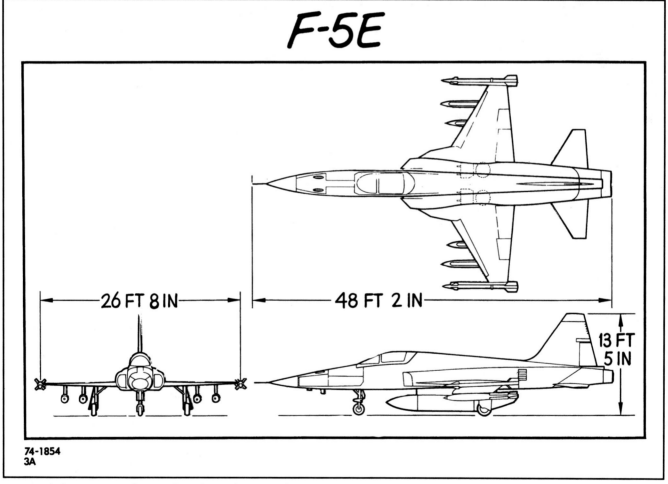

Essential dimensions of span, length, and height for the F-5E are presented in this three-view line art from Northrop. (Craig Kaston collection)

Two Top Gun F-5Es awaited training sorties at Naval Air Station Miramar, near San Diego, California, when photographed in January 1980.

Small but mighty, the J85 engine has evolved to provide the F-5 series with increased capabilities. Photographed at NAS Fallon, Nevada, in October 2005.

trim changes automatically as the flaps are moved. Using a flap lever on the throttle quadrant or a thumb switch on the right-hand throttle can actuate the flaps.

With the maneuver flap system, the F-5E (and F-model) central air data computer (CADC) analyzes flight conditions and selects the most appropriate of three maneuver settings when requested by the pilot. With the auto flap system, the CADC prompts flap settings for all phases of flight from takeoff to landing. However, pilots of F-5Es and F-5Fs equipped with auto flap systems are cautioned to disengage the auto flap setting during en-route cruise because turbulence may change the angle of attack (AOA), prompting the auto system to reposition the flaps, which could inadvertently decrease fuel economy.[118] The F-5E's flaps are powered by AC electric motors. The flight controls are hydraulically actuated and have redundancy.

The E-model's frontal area is bigger by more than 14 percent, at 21.3 square feet versus 18.6 square feet in the F-5A. This includes an increase in the inlet size to 3.4 square feet on the F-5E instead of 2.1 square feet on the F-5A.

If the bulked-up F-5E airframe increased friction drag, Northrop designers introduced a cruise flap setting (called 0/8 for 0 degrees leading edge and 8 degrees trailing edge) that offset much of this. There is more to the sleek appearance of the F-5 than merely a sense of aesthetics. Northrop engineers were keenly aware of a mathematical concept called fineness ratio (fuselage length-to-diameter ratio). Fineness ratio impacts drag experienced at supersonic speeds; in essence, longer fuselages are better. When the F-5E's cross-section enlarged slightly, its length had to stretch in order to preserve the fineness ratio enjoyed by the earlier F-5A. The fineness ratio of the F-5E is 9.7 compared with 9.8 for the F-5A–a mere one percent decrease. The F-5E's extra thrust more than compensated for this.

All of the air superiority enhancements to the airframe of the F-5E are complemented by an integrated fire-control system that uses radar and a computing gun-sight system to help the pilot put 20-mm rounds or AIM-9 missiles on target in an air-to-air fight. The lead computing sight analyzes target range signals from the radar, airspeed and angle-of-attack data from the CADC, plus acceleration and turn rate information from the gyro lead computer to give the pilot an aiming reference on the glass heads-up optical sight.

Tiger in the Sky

First flight of a dedicated F-5E (71-1417) was 11 August 1972 at Edwards AFB, at the hands of Northrop test pilot Hank Chouteau.

The F-5E was grounded from 19 September to 16 December 1972, due to problems with J85 compressor blades. When the F-5E resumed flights in December, it was with a reduced engine-operating envelope initially. Meanwhile, F-5A 63-8372 hosted the production E-model fire-control system in flight tests that expanded its operational envelope in low-altitude flight. The second F-5E (71-1418) flew for the first time on 29 December 1972.[119]

Over an 11-day period in February 1973, Joint Test Force (JTF) pilots flew a 10-flight Air Force Preliminary Evaluation (AFPE) in the first F-5E (71-1417). According to a contemporary F-5E JTF document: "Results showed the handling qualities to be equivalent to or slightly better than the F-5A. Major deficiencies were excessive nose-gear retraction time following hiked takeoffs and fuel balance warning system deficiency."[120] (Hiked takeoffs referred to the use of a two-position nose landing gear strut that could be elevated, or hiked, for takeoff to decrease ground roll, and shortened for taxiing to promote better visibility for the pilot.)

F-5E tests continued to validate the Tiger II's fire-control system's operational capability at all altitudes. By March 1973, six F-5Es comprised the test force. That

Twin throttles of an F-5E are grouped at the left of the photo, just to the left of the black-and-yellow striped ejection seat handle. Photo taken October 2005 at NAS Fallon, Nevada.

month, most operating restrictions on the F-5's J85-21 engines were removed.[121] By the end of April, the J85-21 engine completed Model Qualification Tests (MQT), enabling the F-5E's engines to be requalified for flight without restrictions.

The F-5E achieved airspeed just above Mach 1.6 during level acceleration at 36,000 feet MSL (Mean Sea

F-5E ejection seat is intended to depart a stricken aircraft after the canopy is jettisoned, although a thick blade at the top of the seat is placed to shatter the plastic canopy if it is in the way during an ejection sequence. Photo taken October 2005 at Navy squadron VFC-13 in Fallon, Nevada.

Level; the altitude above sea level) on 5 April 1973. During this period, Air Force gunnery flights using dart-towed targets saw hits scored. Marginally successful results were logged in 54 attempted engagements of the

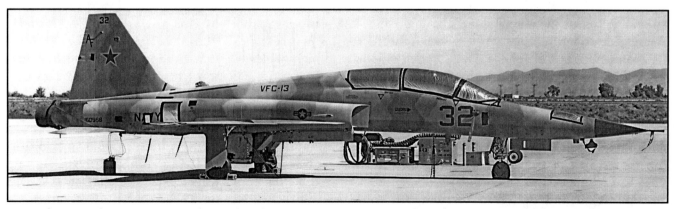

One of VFC-13's aggressor F-5Fs was placed in temporary storage on the ramp at NAS Fallon, Nevada, when photographed in October 2005.

Dotted lines on top of F-5E wing enclose no-step areas. Streamlined teardrop fixture to the left of national insignia is red navigation light housing. Photo taken 12 October 2005 at NAS Fallon, Nevada.

runway overrun barrier cable by an F-5E fitted with an arresting hook, with 43 successful engagements. Hook bounce and dynamics of the cable were cited as reasons for the less than perfect performance; during the tests the arresting hook damper was modified in an effort to diminish the tendency of the hook to bounce when contacting the pavement.[122]

By late 1973, F-5Es were entering foreign air force inventories. Activities of the F-5E JTF included testing and evaluation to meet needs peculiar to specific customer countries. In July 1974, test pilots flew an F-5E in a steep 11-degree glide slope approach to landing (versus the normal three-degree glide slope). This prepared the JTF commander, Lt. Col. John H. Taylor, to ferry an aircraft to mountainous Switzerland so that country could evaluate the Tiger II in their operational environment. The JTF aircraft were not used solely for testing; during the last half of 1974, F-5E 72-0386 was refurbished to production configuration and delivered to McClellan AFB near Sacramento, California, for overseas shipment.[123]

The following year, F-5E 71-1421 departed the test force and joined the 425th Tactical Fighter Training Squadron (TFTS) at Williams AFB, Arizona. In the last half of 1976, the first F-5E, 71-1417, was handed over to the Tactical Air Command as well.

Flight tests of improved radar, hosted in the traditionally radarless F-5A (63-8372) continued in the summer of 1974. Plans by the end of the year included installing a flatter cross section (ogive) radome.[124] Several airframe shape modifications, including the leading edge extension (LEX), fuselage widening, and ogive (sharknose) radome all contributed to make the F-5E a more capable dogfighter than its precursor A-model, especially at high angles of attack.

Nonetheless, although the F-5A was notoriously spin-resistant, the F-5E showed it could be put into a potentially catastrophic spin; during spin testing, on 6 November 1975, an F-5E entered a spin from which it could not be recovered before passing through the mandatory spin chute deployment altitude of 30,000 feet. Deployment of the aft-mounted spin chute stopped the spin. Subsequently, the F-5 testers lowered the spin chute altitude to 25,000 feet in an effort to give the pilot more time to see if pilotage could be used to come out of a spin.[125] During early 1976, the F-5E spin program coaxed three spins, two of which were recoverable by application of flight controls; only one required deployment of the spin chute.[126] By the end of the 70-flight spin susceptibility test, aircraft 71-1417 performed 428 maneuvers resulting in a number of departures from controlled flight, only two of which required use of the spin chute for recovery.[127]

The two-place F-5F received its own spin susceptibility test program from August to November 1976 with aircraft 73-00891. In 197 test maneuvers, the aircraft departed controlled flight 21 times, according to Air Force documentation. "Recovery from all inverted spins was possible with aerodynamic controls," an Air Force report explained. "The spin chute was required in three instances to recover from erect spins."[128]

A Tiger Built for Two

In April 1973, a full-scale development program got underway for the F-5F two-seat version of the powerful new Tiger II. While packing only one M39 20-mm cannon in its modified forward fuselage, the F-5F retained the rest of the E-model's combat capabilities. As with the earlier two-seat F-5B, the F-model could fulfill a training role in addition to flying combat for smaller air forces. First flight of an F-5F was on 25 September 1974. Northrop received the go-ahead for full production of the F-5F for the FMS

(Foreign Military Sales) program on 30 May 1975.

During early JTF flight evaluations of the two-seat F-5F, the F-model's longer fuselage with its center of gravity moved ahead of the location on the F-5E was said to make the F-model only marginally compatible with a single-seat F-5E in formation takeoffs and landings. Under consideration at that time was a weight redistribution to move the F-5F's center of gravity aft, and a change to give the F-5F greater horizontal stabilator authority.[129]

International Flavor

The F-5F test force at Edwards AFB included at least one example earmarked for the Iranian Air Force upon completion of its test career. F-5 E/F testing included a program tailored to the needs of foreign customers. The Saudi Arabian Air Force's program in 1976 was called Peace Hawk IV. It involved F-5Es and F-models, including reconnaissance versions. F-5E 71-1418 flew in the Peace Hawk IV program, performing Maverick missile operations and providing data on the nature of airflow disturbances caused by small streamlined radar warning receiver (RWR) antennas mounted to the fuselage. (As with so much of the F-5's history, devices evaluated for one foreign customer often became common to many users' aircraft.) Documentation from the F-5 Joint Test Force at Edwards AFB indicates F-5F 73-00889, used in Peace Hawk IV tests, underwent a wing replacement "with a new higher strength assembly" in the first half of 1976.[130]

Even while tests were underway on F-5Es and –Fs in configurations destined for Saudi Arabia, other demonstration flights were made for countries including Singapore. F-5E 71-1418, the second E-model, tested

Close-up photos show F-5E inlet details, and shape of late-design leading edge extension LEX W-6, photographed 12 October 2005 at NAS Fallon, Nevada.

Aggressor F-5E with Navy squadron VFC-13 carries inert wingtip AIM-9 missiles with sensors to indicate probability of missile hits, as photographed in October 2005.

F-5E of Navy squadron VFC-13 photographed in October 2005 retained 20-mm cannons in its nose; their removal necessitates addition of ballast to maintain proper center of gravity.

an anti-skid brake system intended for Swiss F-5s. During this test period in the last half of 1976, aircraft 71-1418 also used a modified LEX that improved lateral directional stability in the region of stall angle of attack. The aircraft concurrently demonstrated an auto-flap system that showed some advantages in maneuvering flight, but which proved unsuitable during formation flight "due to the frequent flap shifts as a result of small AoA (angle of attack) changes," according to Air Force Flight Test Center document.[131]

F-5F 73-00889 made three live Maverick missile firings in the last half of 1976. That October, an AVQ-27 laser designator set was installed in the rear cockpit for tests, with airborne lasing performed by December.[132]

The wide array of F-5E and F-model testing was characterized in an F-5 JTF report covering the first half of 1977 that inventoried the accom-

View of left-hand mainwheel well of an F-5E at NAS Fallon, Nevada, in October 2005 reveals details of construction and plumbing.

Far Left: Extended left-hand speed brake of an F-5E occupies fuselage undersurface immediately ahead of left main-wheel well, as photographed in October 2005 at NAS Fallon, Nevada.

White painted left main gear strut of an F-5E was photographed in October 2005 on the VFC-13 tarmac at NAS Fallon, Nevada.

plishments of test F-5s by tail number, including the following highlights:[133]

F-5E 71-1418: Tested nosewheel steering actuator link loads in support of an overseas F-5E mishap investigation, and evaluated loads and vibrations associated with Maverick missile single rail launcher during missile launch.

F-5E 71-1419: Primary test vehicle for Block III fire control radar fixes.

F-5E 75-00462: Production verification of chaff/flare countermeasures dispenser and F-5E AGM-65 Maverick missile system, as well as Block III radar fixes.

F-5E 75-00463: Used to evaluate radar performance during gunfire missions and high-load flight operations where radar problems have been experienced.

Closed auxiliary engine inlet louvers are visible to the left of NAVY lettering on this Tiger II of VFC-13 at NAS Fallon, Nevada, in October 2005.

JP-8 jet fuel sump on an F-5E drains into a fuel can for disposal at NAS Fallon, Nevada, in October 2005. Striped black-and-white tailhook rests on ventral centerline.

There's not much spring in the strut when the F-5 Tiger II shortens its nosegear to enhance pilot visibility during taxiing.

F-5E 75-00472 performed air-to-air gunnery missions for initial operational test and evaluation (IOT&E) efforts before delivery to Saudi Arabia.

F-5F 73-00889 worked on radar fixes and Maverick missile demonstrations. The aircraft was restored to production configuration and toured the Paris Air Show and other European destinations before returning to Edwards and its subsequent destination, Tactical Air Command.

F-5F 75-00712 verified the radar warning receiver system, the Maverick missile system, and worked on radar fixes, among its tasks for the reporting period.

F-5F 75-00713 had the unusual duty of production verification tests of an F-5 rocket assisted take-

Removal of 20-mm cannons from the noses of F-5 Tiger IIs requires the substitution of ballast like these heavy metal plates to maintain proper balance of the aircraft. Photographed 12 October 2005 at NAS Fallon, Nevada.

Ex-Swiss air force F-5E flown by U.S. Navy squadron VFC-13 has black radar warning receivers (RWR) on the nose and tail, as photographed on 12 October 2005.

off (RATO) system, aerial refueling with a KC-130F tanker, and the reconnaissance nose system. Early refueling tests pointed out potential sideslip problems with the F-5F refueling probe installed.

F-5F 73-00891 carried airframe modifications with significant implications. The jet was flown to evaluate spin susceptibility and high angle-of-attack (AoA) handling qualities with a modified wing LEX identified as W-6, plus a sharknose flattened radome. Seven flights used only the LEX; 13 flights incorporated the new LEX and the sharknose. Directional stability at very high AoAs improved and spin susceptibility diminished.

Triple-tone gray F-5F of VFC-13 at NAS Fallon, Nevada, is one of a handful of two-seaters the aggressor squadron maintained as of this writing.

F-5E 71-1420 and F-5A 63-8372 remained in flyable storage during this period.

In the last half of 1977, sorties pitting an F-5E against an F-5F and others involving a T-38 adversary were flown with the F-5s in two configurations—with and without air refueling probe installed. In the clean configuration, the single-seat F-5E's performance was slightly improved, while the two-seat F-5F "showed a significant improvement without the probe," according to a TAC F-5 report.[134]

Recce F-5s

The F-5A could be built with an angular shark-like nose for cameras and sensors, giving allied customers a nimble reconnaissance jet compatible with their front-line fighter. The resulting RF-5A served in small numbers (about 120 were built) with several international customers. Typical RF-5A variants were dedicated with that configuration; Canadian recon models could swap the camera nose for a fighter nose more readily. With the advent of the improved single-seat F-5E, Northrop revisited the reconnaissance concept in the mid-1970s.

As with the RF-5A that preceded it, the RF-5E would represent only a

F-5Fs were fitted with wing fences as seen on an example flying with Navy squadron VFC-13 in October 2005.

Tiger II nose bay hinges downward to provide access to avionics.

Looking up the business end of a pair of J85 engines, it is evident the close pairing of the two powerplants results in relatively small amounts of asymmetrical thrust in the Tiger II if uneven power is applied.

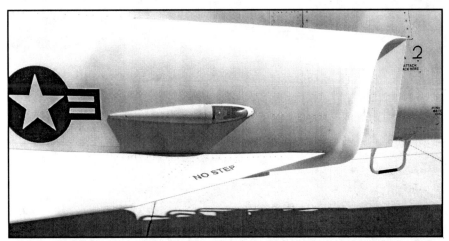

Some of Navy squadron VFC-13's Tiger IIs have the older, smaller style leading edge extension, as photographed on this F-5E on 12 October 2005.

small portion of any foreign country's air force. The U.S. Air Force had no plans to obtain its own RF-5Es. The cost of developing a unique RF-5E would be too much for any one foreign customer to absorb. With these realities, Northrop embarked on a plan to develop the RF-5E using company funds, hoping to sell enough of this improved reconnaissance aircraft to justify the cost.[135]

The RF-5E was designed under the premise that its basic high-speed performance would be much better served if the recon systems were housed within the sleek fuselage instead of being pod-mounted. The RF-5E was also intended to retain one of the F-5E's two nose-mounted 20-mm Colt cannons, as well as the wingtip-mounted AIM-9 Sidewinder missiles and the ability to carry other external stores, to enhance the aircraft's overall utility for its small user air forces. The initial RF-5E development was approved by Air Force headquarters in March 1978 with the stipulation it be done at no cost to the government. Northrop leased F-5E number 71-01420 to be the testbed RF-5E. Northrop also paid for limited Air Force participation as a monitor to the RF-5E demonstration program.[136]

The RF-5E's derivation from the F-5E was described in an Air Force report: "The F-5E is a single-place, supersonic reconnaissance/fighter aircraft powered by two J85-GE-21 turbojet engines of 5,000 lbs thrust each. The RF-5E Tigereye reconnaissance version of the F-5 incorporates structural and aerodynamic changes to the forward fuselage to

Removing J85 engines from F-5s is a manual operation aided by a simple overhead monorail device to transfer the engine from the fuselage to the engine dolly.

View looking aft through the boattail section of a Tiger II shows construction details.

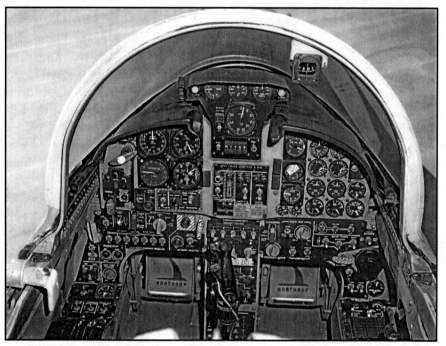

F-5F number 891's front cockpit was photographed in September 1976. (AFFTC/HO collection)

Coiled tubing feeds jet fuel to the afterburner on a J85-21 engine used in the F-5E and F-models.

permit installation of various palletized sensor systems in the nose. Other systems incorporated to facilitate the reconnaissance mission include an inertial navigation system, radar altimeter, improved environmental control system, integrated sensor control computer, and television... video viewfinder system."[137]

A 1979 Northrop technical article elaborated on the Tigereye's capabilities: "The RF-5E collects photographic intelligence at low,

medium, and high altitudes and infrared (IR) intelligence at low altitudes. System components consist of a forward-looking frame camera, vertical panoramic variable scan cameras, IR line scanner sensor mounted in one camera station, a television viewfinder camera and display with auxiliary controls..." A button on the control stick operated the cameras and sensors. The special recon nose for the RF-5E added about eight inches to the length of a basic F-5E.[138]

Northrop anticipated different countries would have different reconnaissance requirements. Of three pallets in the special nose section, pallet 1 was considered a standard configuration common to most users, while pallets 2 and 3 could host differing equipment as required. The standardized pallet 1 was fitted with three sensors for low to medium altitude reconnaissance missions. A KA-95B panoramic camera in this pallet, with a 12-inch focal length lens, was optimal

Left side view of the cockpit of F-5F 891 shows details of throttles and side panels. (AFFTC/HO collection)

record detail from about 200 to 3,000 feet. In daylight, this IR scanner could detect otherwise camouflaged targets by the heat they produced. It was said to be so sensitive that it could "detect temperature differences of approximately one-half degree Celsius in the far IR spectral region," according to Northrop literature.[139]

A separate compartment in the extreme nose of the RF-5E was intended for a KS-87B oblique camera for forward oblique photography along the line of flight at low and medium altitudes. This camera was accessed on the ground by unlatching the tip of the nose and sliding it forward on rails. Combat mapping could be accomplished by relocating the KS-87B camera to a vertical offset position in pallet 1, while retaining the KA-95B or KA-56E camera in that pallet.[140]

Pallet 2 could carry several types of cameras including a KA-93B to give detailed panoramas from 10,000 up to 50,000 feet. This camera could also be mounted for medium-range standoff

for capturing detailed images from altitudes between 2,500 and 20,000 feet. A KA-56E panoramic camera was intended for cross-track scanning at low altitudes—from 100 to 5,000 feet, according to a Northrop description. The third sensor in pallet 1 was the infrared RS-710 line scanner with a 3.4-inch focal length reflective optical system. This device could be used day or night and had the ability to

Removal of a Tiger II's engines at NAS Fallon, Nevada, in October 2005 provides a glimpse inside the fuselage engine bay.

photography in left or right oblique positioning. This enabled reconnaissance to be accomplished as far as 14 nautical miles offset from a target, with vehicle-size targets being recognizable at that distance, according to Northrop. Pallets 2 and 3 could be configured with cameras to sweep across the flight track with coverage extending 41 miles, or with a KA-108(MOD) camera that was shown to be effective over a distances of 30 miles. (Although, in practice the KS-147A with a 66-inch focal length lens replaced the KA-108.)[141] The sensor suite on the RF-5E had semi-automatic camera control. Inputs from the aircraft's inertial navigation system (INS) and radar altimeter helped ensure the cameras recorded correct views. The onboard television camera, mounted in the bottom of the fuselage ahead of the pilot's feet, had a six-power zoom lens to give the pilot a variable forward and downward field of view to aid in target location. The video camera could also help the pilot to watch, and correct if need be, his aircraft's line of flight during mapping runs.[142]

The U.S. Air Force had an awkward position in the RF-5E program. The service made it clear that no RF-5Es would be purchased for USAF use, and yet the Air Force discharged an obligation to make sure the product Northrop wanted to sell to allies worked as advertised. As explained in an AFFTC (Air Force Flight Test Center) report on the aircraft: "The RF-5E test and evaluation is a contractor funded development

A pair of F-models in the test program circa August 1975 evaluated the dart target tow rig attached to aircraft 891. (AFFTC/HO collection)

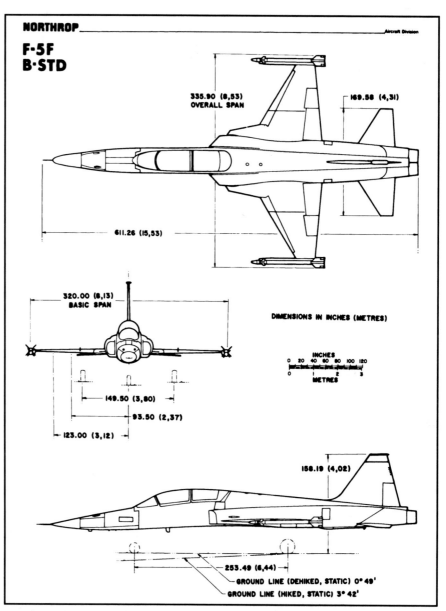

Northrop three-view of F-5F was measured in inches and meters, a convenience for some international customers. (Craig Kaston collection)

Dimensioned front view of the F-5E shows wings have no dihedral, while horizontal stabilizers have negative dihedral of four degrees. Washout of airfoil at wingtips gives missile mounts a nose-down angle. (Northrop via Craig Kaston collection)

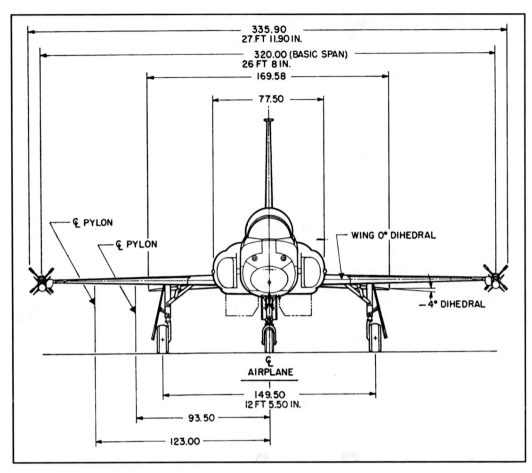

Variations in nose and cockpit geometry give the front view of the two-seat F-5F subtle differences from the shape of the F-5E. (Northrop via Craig Kaston collection)

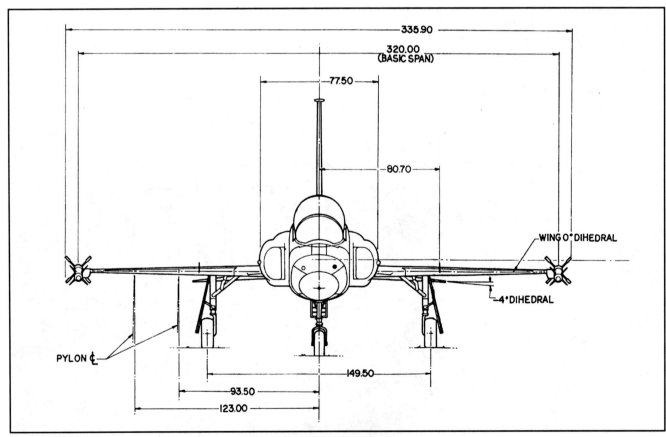

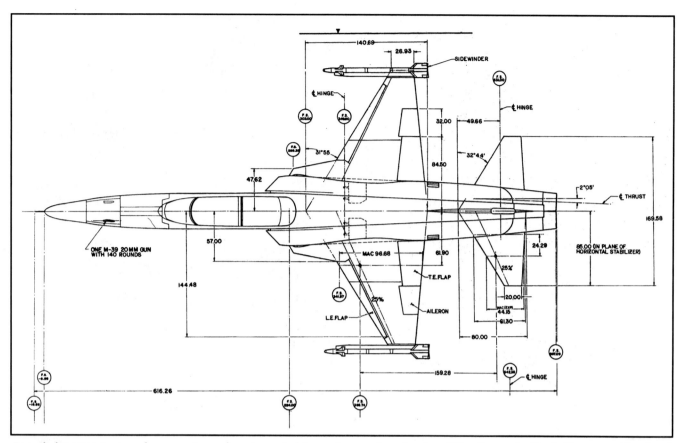

Detailed F-5F top view shows engine exhausts canted inward toward each other. (Northrop via Craig Kaston collection)

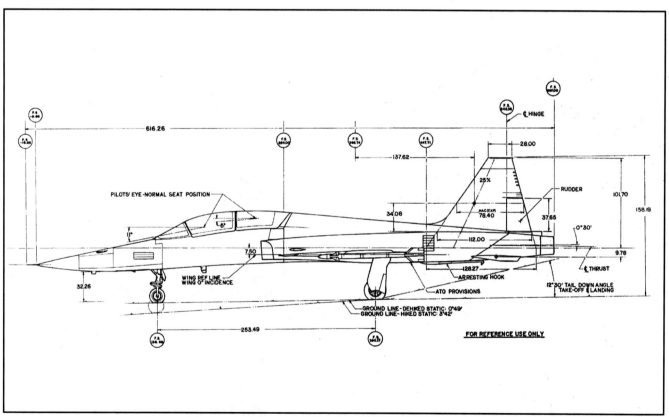

Side elevation of the F-5F shows back seat pilot has higher line of sight than front seat pilot; a convenience for training. (Northrop via Craig Kaston collection)

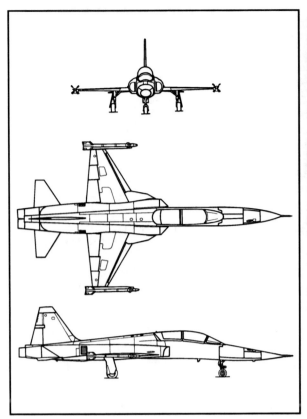

During tests, the rear cockpit of F-5F 891 was photographed 2 September 1976 with brown sheetmetal panels baffling the rudder pedal cutouts in the instrument panel. (AFFTC/HO collection)

Left: Simple F-5F three-view drawing depicts early small leading edge extension. (Northrop via Craig Kaston collection)

Side view of F-5F number 713 shows right-hand installation of refueling probe. (AFFTC/HO collection)

Special colors including an orange vertical fin and black-and-white wing helped trackers observe F-5F number 75-0713 during its flight test program over Edwards Air Force Base in September 1980. Package atop engine exhausts is spin chute to be deployed if a spin proved otherwise unrecoverable. It was seldom needed. This aircraft later went to Saudi Arabia. (AFFTC/HO collection)

program. The USAF has been directed to serve as executive agent for the program and AFSC (Air Force Systems Command) has been charged to ensure that the aircraft meets USAF quality standards. The AFFTC will accomplish USAF flight testing and will participate in those areas of the flight test program designed to verify that the aircraft is safe, is airworthy, and meets the design flight characteristics. A major flight test effort by AFFTC is not required." The Air Force position was, "...the results of such testing

Resplendent in metallic silver paint, F-5F bearing U.S. Navy Bureau Number 160966 was photographed at the Top Gun school at NAS Miramar in January 1980. Large U.S. national insignia blankets the right main landing gear door.

Engine work on a Navy F-5F at NAS Miramar in January 1980 illustrates the benefit of a canted removable boattail section that allows the rudder to remain attached to the fuselage, while the canted boattail seam gains considerable additional access to the J85 engines.

Photos of an F-5F going vertical show the characteristic camber to the forward fuselage. (AFFTC/HO collection)

will not imply that the systems are necessarily suitable for USAF operations."[143]

Developmental test and evaluation (DT&E) was a prime task of test forces at Edwards AFB. For the RF-5E, the DT&E program was Northrop-run, with some Air Force participation and oversight. The overall objective was "to perform a limited airworthiness evaluation on the RF-5E as a tactical reconnaissance aircraft," that would verify company performance claims, according to an AFFTC summary. For the DT&E effort that followed Northrop's earlier proof of concept, the aircraft tested was the second production RF-5E, one of two ordered through the Foreign Military Sales (FMS) program by Malaysia. It was to be delivered to the customer at the conclusion of the tests.

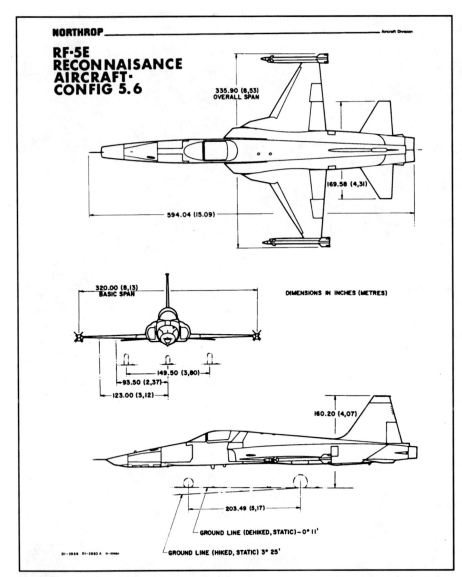

NORTHROP _____ Aircraft Division

RF-5E RECONNAISANCE AIRCRAFT· CONFIG 5.6

335.90 (8,53) OVERALL SPAN

594.04 (15,09)

169.58 (4,31)

320.00 (8,13) BASIC SPAN

DIMENSIONS IN INCHES (METRES)

149.50 (3,80)

93.50 (2,37)

123.00 (3,12)

160.20 (4,07)

203.49 (5,17)

GROUND LINE (DEHIKED, STATIC) – 0° 11'

GROUND LINE (HIKED, STATIC) 3° 25'

DI-2959 DI-2963 A DI-2964

Northrop three-view depiction of single-place RF-5E recon jet shows nose contours modified to accommodate cameras. (Craig Kaston collection)

11420

U.S. AIR FORCE

End of the Line

By late November 1986, the F-5E/F production line at Hawthorne, California, was down to its last seven aircraft. Northrop built 2,603 F-5s, including 1,399 E- and F-models. The F-5 would fly on for many years—as of this writing, the U.S. Navy's adversary squadron VFC-13 at NAS Fallon is receiving upgraded F-5N models refurbished from ex-Swiss Air Force F-5Es.

Friendly Foe

The F-5's traditional stance as an outsider to operational U.S. military units rendered it uniquely suitable when the Navy, followed by the Air Force, wanted a capable jet adversary to train fighter pilots in combat tactics. Believing dogfight training would be more realistic with dissimilar aircraft, the U.S. military's employment of F-5s was a natural. The Navy established its vaunted Top Gun program in 1969, initially with

In flight is the best way to view the photo-reconnaissance nose-modifications on RF-5E Tigereye number 420. Aircraft had small leading edge extensions. Photo taken 22 January 1979. (AFFTC/HO collection)

Silver-painted RF-5E reconnaissance variant, number 71-1420, was prototype example. (AFFTC/HO collection)

WARBIRD**TECH** SERIES

A-4 Skyhawks, later supplemented by T-38s. F-5Es and -Fs became the ultimate Northrop fighters employed in this role by the Navy. Use of Navy F-5s waned in the 1980s and 1990s, with F-16Ns and Israeli F-21A Kfirs doing the job. As of this writing, the Navy's VFC-13 at Fallon, Nevada, is bulking up its use of F-5Es and F-5Fs with upgraded sharknosed F-5Ns, modified from ex-Swiss Air Force F-5Es for the dissimilar combat training role. The squadron also has a detachment at Key West, Florida. The Marine Corps operates F-5s for dissimilar combat training at Yuma, Arizona, in squadron VMFT-401 as of this writing.

The U.S. Air Force also realized the need for dissimilar aircraft combat training, and began using T-38s in the role of aggressors at Nellis AFB, Nevada, in 1972. The T-38 was less desirable as an aggressor fighter than a full-fledged F-5E. When E-models originally intended for South Vietnam became available after the fall of the Saigon government in 1975, numerous F-5Es became available to the U.S. Air Force's aggressor squadrons. In a Cold War era with American assets stationed around the world, the Air Force also established aggressor squadrons in England and the Philippines to test the mettle of overseas USAF units. By 1990, its F-5s showing the ravages of continual air combat engagements, a USAF switch to F-16s was blunted when the overall aggressor program was terminated. A cadre of F-16s remained at Nellis to provide aggressor services during Red Flag exercises there.[144]

Line art depicted camera placement in RF-5E configuration, with 20-mm cannon lightly drawn in upper nose area just ahead of windscreen. (Northrop via Craig Kaston collection)

Angular facets of RF-5E nose provided optically true glass apertures for cameras pointing in several directions. (Northrop via Craig Kaston collection)

Altered nose contours of Tigereye E-model recon version are evident in this in-flight close-up photo taken 22 January 1979. (AFFTC/HO collection)

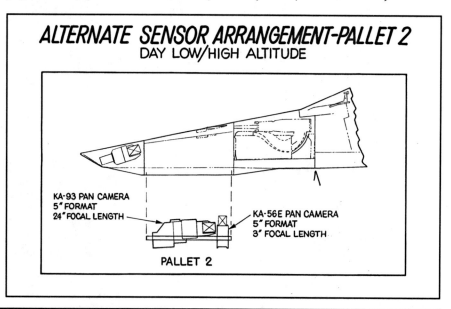

ALTERNATE SENSOR ARRANGEMENT-PALLET 2
DAY LOW/HIGH ALTITUDE

KA-93 PAN CAMERA
5" FORMAT
24" FOCAL LENGTH

KA-56E PAN CAMERA
5" FORMAT
3" FOCAL LENGTH

PALLET 2

F-20 TIGERSHARK

One of aviation's oldest arguments pits the supposed safety merits of multi-engine aircraft against the small size and simplicity of single-engine variants. And yet, the increasing reliability of aero engines, possibly coupled with the fact that combat aircraft are all too often destroyed by catastrophic damage that would negate any number of engines, argues favorably for single-engine designs if the sole engine is up to the task.

After years of capitalizing on the neat package provided by two GE J85 turbojets in all models of the F-5, Northrop made a major shift to a single-engine version, initially tagged F-5G, and ultimately redesignated F-20. By the late 1970s, ascendancy of the small single-engine General Dynamics F-16 was apparent. After contemplating a single-engine F-5 derivative for Taiwan, Northrop pushed ahead with design studies in 1980. Powerplant was to be the GE F404 low-bypass turbofan, which was said to give the Northrop fighter freedom from any kind of throttle restrictions because the engine was free of compressor stalls or flameouts in the F-5G.

The F-5G first flew 30 August 1982 as Northrop pilot Russ Scott eased the new fighter off the Edwards AFB runway in the company of an F-5F chase plane. The jet achieved Mach 1.04 on its first flight. An early goal of the Northrop flight test program was to clear enough of the F-5G's flight envelope as soon as possible to permit its demonstration to potential customers. The single-engine fighter bore the name Tigershark on its first flight.[145]

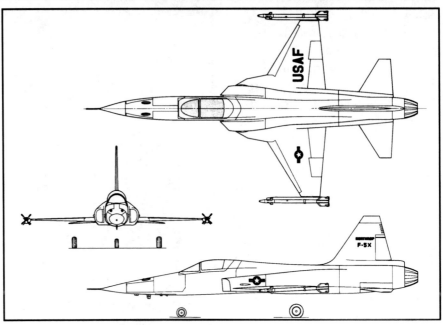

Northrop's early deliberations on a single-engine F-5 derivative yielded this three-view concept labeled F-5X, designed around the GE F404 powerplant. Many subtle changes, from inlet design to the so-called "file cabinet" at the base of the vertical fin of the final F-20, would evolve over the life of the program. (Northrop via Craig Kaston collection)

Evolving sophistication of cockpit instrumentation suite is evident in this view of an F-5G/F-20 configuration featuring use of flat screen and heads-up displays as well as some traditional round gauges. (AFFTC/HO collection)

The Tigershark was developed into a formidable weapons system, toting up to six Sidewinder air-to-air missiles. Capable of carrying 8,100 lbs of external armament and fuel tanks, the Tigershark could heft more than 6,800 lbs of armament for air-to-ground sorties. The familiar pair of internal 20-mm cannons remained in the nose of the new Northrop.[146] The Tigershark was built beefy enough to withstand 9 Gs—nine times the force of gravity. It used the flattened "sharknose" also added to some F-5Es to permit maneuvering at higher angles of attack than some fighters.

Area Rule is More Than Aesthetics

Although the F-5G maintained the tenets of area rule in its design, the evidence is not nearly as clear as in the classically curvy F-5A and T-38. Area rule, as developed and explained by NASA engineer Richard Whitcomb, mathematically dictates the proper fuselage cross section at any given point in relation to the wing, to diminish the effects of drag induced by the shock wave formed as an aircraft passes through the transonic region into supersonic flight. The F-5A is a stunning visualization of area rule, its fuselage narrowing where it abuts the wing to help neutralize the transonic shockwave drag. Even the wingtip fuel tanks of the F-5A and F-5B employ area rule where their inboard surfaces meet the wings. This reduced transonic buffeting and longitudinal instabilities encountered in wind tunnel tests of a bullet-shaped tip tank without area rule.

Using Whitcomb's principles, Northrop designers originally sculpted the F-5/T-38 airframe to meet Mach 1.0 standards. High-speed wind tunnel tests performed before an aircraft was built suggested a better value would be to design the early airframes within area rule guidelines for Mach 1.15, resulting in the slightly different aspect of the airframes as built.

With the advent of the heftier and more powerful F-5E, area rule was still in evidence, albeit perhaps not as dramatically as with the F-5A. By the time the single-engine F-5G/F-20 was designed, the sides of the fuselage had lost nearly all of their pinch-waisted geometry. Yet as the fuselage tapered in toward the aft to accommodate the single exhaust nozzle of the F-5G's engine, even this taper helped conserve the physical laws of area rule. Additionally, a housing at the base of the F-5G vertical fin that was unique to this model added geometry that helped fulfill the cross-section requirements of area rule. The F-5G's remarkable 18,000 lbs of engine thrust—more than twice that of an F-5A—might also be expected to muscle the airframe through the rigors of transonic flight better than early-generation J85s could.

The Name Game

The F-5G, though clearly inheriting genes from the Northrop pool, was substantially a different jet than previous F-5s. For the first time, an aircraft from this family tree was

Simplified exploded view of early F-5G concept shows design similarities and differences from standard twin-engine F-5 precursors. (Northrop via Craig Kaston collection)

Near the 35th anniversary of first breaking the sound barrier, retired Brig. Gen. Chuck Yeager flew the bright new F-5G on 13 October 1982 at Edwards Air Force Base. (AFFTC/HO collection)

considered a Mach 2 fighter. Its thrust was greater than its weight in some conditions, and it was said to reach 40,000 feet 2.3 minutes after brake release. This new Northrop fighter was also competing against the F-16 for foreign sales. Whatever the reason for changing its designation, it probably didn't hurt the Northrop fighter's image when its nomenclature was bumped up from F-5G to F-20—vaulting its number ahead of the competing, and older, F-16.

The second company-funded Tigershark, now known as the F-20, flew nearly a year later on 26 August 1983, reaching Mach 1.2 and 45,000 feet on its inaugural sortie. This aircraft introduced a higher and longer clear canopy to enhance pilot visibility by 50 percent in rear quarters. Three single-seaters, technically designated F-20As, were built by Northrop to undertake flight-testing and marketing missions.

The F-20's original stated purpose, as a follow-on foreign sales aircraft to augment the already successful F-5 series, appeared to be supported by actions of the Carter presidency which sought to restrict foreign sales of sophisticated hardware like the F-16. American government officials at that time envisioned a new export fighter with performance somewhere between that of the F-5E and a full-up USAF F-16. To garner that export market, General Dynamics offered a diluted version of the F-16 while Northrop proceeded with its hot-rod single-engine derivative of the F-5. The time seemed right for Northrop to capitalize on the foreign sales it already enjoyed, which would see more than 2,600 aircraft

The GE F404 engine gave the F-20 performance beyond that attainable in classic F-5s, and warranted the switch from two engines to a single engine. (AFFTC/HO collection)

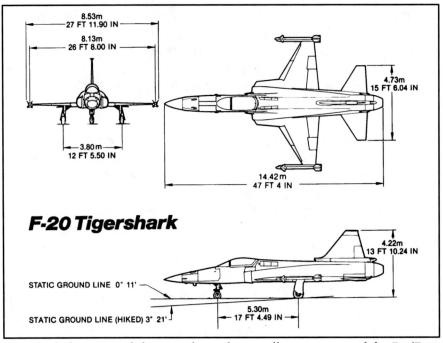

Tigershark dimensioned drawing shows the overall compactness of the F-5/F-20 family. Tigersharks retained the hiked nosegear strut made popular on earlier F-5s for enhanced takeoff performance. (Northrop via Craig Kaston collection)

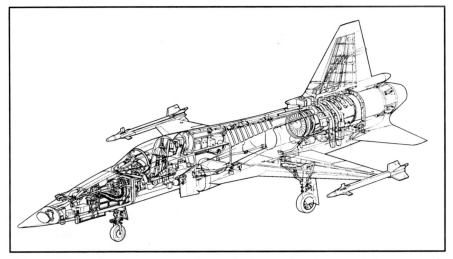

Crisp F-20 line drawing cutaway shows the internal and external changes needed to accommodate the single GE F404 engine. Drawing predates finished F-20, and shows aft horizontal tail fairing not applied to actual aircraft. (Northrop via Craig Kaston collection)

Striking planview of F-20 in flight over the Mojave Desert shows evolved leading-edge extensions that helped the Tigershark remain maneuverable at high angles of attack. (AFFTC/HO collection)

in the F-5 series built for 32 nations. But the premise of limiting advanced hardware sales to foreign countries went away with the incoming Reagan presidency. Now the "intermediate" F-5G/F-20 would have to compete with whatever the competition had. Northrop upped the ante at this point, enhancing their fighter's navigation system.[147]

Northrop pilots enthusiastically praised the upgraded F-20 as a match for contemporary F-16s, but the die may already have been cast by earlier marketing of the Tigershark as an intermediate-level fighter. Many foreign customers expressed a preference for the F-16. Northrop's team figured they could offer the F-20 to foreign customers at about 70 percent of the cost of an F-16, while delivering perhaps 95 percent of the performance of that competitor.

By early 1985, Northrop was cutting metal for the fourth F-20, intending to equip this aircraft with the latest production upgrades that the company hoped would make the Tigershark a world-beater. Among the changes planned was a larger antenna for the AN/APG-67(V) radar, said to improve its abilities to

detect a fighter the size of a MiG-23 in a head-on approach. The radar changes necessitated some nose recontouring on the fourth F-20.[148]

Plans called for the fourth Tigershark to use an increased afterburner thrust of 18,000 lbs instead of the 17,000 lbs available on earlier F-20s. Internal fuel tankage was to be increased by an additional 650 lbs by using an integral structure. External fuel tanks were again to be upsized, from 275 gallons to 330 gallons.

The fourth F-20's fighter maneuvering capabilities were to be enhanced by a redesign of the leading and trailing edge maneuvering flaps to permit faster operation and provide a higher number of automatic position settings. The flap improvements, plus the extra afterburner thrust, were expected to give the fourth F-20 a two-degree-per-second increase in turn rate under some conditions.[149]

Two Losses

Northrop chief test pilot Darrell Cornell died in the crash of the number one F-20 he was demonstrating at Suwon Air Base near Seoul, South

Bright sun on the belly of an F-20 shows the flat bottom, wider than the single engine would require, but desirable to retain optimal fighter flight characteristics especially at high angles of attack. (AFFTC/HO collection)

Korea, 10 October 1984. The Tigershark, serial 82-0062, civil registration N4416T, was on the final leg of a 19-country sales tour when the crash occurred. Subsequent reports, after the mishap investigation, said the F-20's crash was caused by an inverted stall.

On 14 May 1985, the number two F-20 crashed near Goose Bay, Labrador, killing Northrop pilot David Barnes during a practice session for an upcoming European exhibit.

Crashes of pre-production aircraft, even more tragic when lives are lost, have sometimes been brushed aside by subsequent successes. The

F-20 TIGERSHARK PERFORMANCE HIGHLIGHTS

Maximum speed	Mach 2 class
Sea level rate-of-climb	52,800 feet/minute
Combat ceiling	54,700 feet
Takeoff distance (clean)	1,600 feet
Takeoff distance (maximum weight)	4,200 feet
Scramble order to brake release	52 seconds
Time to 40,000 feet from brake release	2.3 minutes
Acceleration time, 0.9M to 1.2M, at 30,000 feet	30 seconds
Sustained turn rate, 0.8M, at 15,000 feet	11.1 degrees/second
Maximum load factor	9g

SPECIFICATIONS

Length	46 feet, 7 inches
Height	13 feet, 10 inches
Wing span	26 feet, 8 inches
Internal fuel	5,050 pounds
Takeoff weight, clean	18,005 pounds
Combat thrust/weight ratio	1.10
Combat weight, 50% fuel	15,480 pounds
Maximum weight	27,500 pounds

ARMAMENT

Two 20mm M-39 cannons, 450 rounds
Two AIM-9 missiles
Five pylons, more than 8,100 pounds external armaments and fuel

Northrop artwork included performance parameters for its Mach 2-class F-20. This drawing conforms more closely to actual aircraft than earlier iterations during development of the Tigershark. (Northrop via AFFTC/HO collection)

classic B-17 Flying Fortress, P-38 Lightning, and P-51 Mustang that achieved so much in World War II all sustained serious mishaps—fatal in the case of the Flying Fortress—early in their development, yet went on to full production. This was not to be the denouement for the F-20 Tigershark.

F-20s for the USAF?

The competition for sales of the F-20 versus the F-16 took a bold new direction in May of 1986 when Northrop submitted a bid to sell 270 Tigersharks to the U.S. Air Force as air defense fighters (ADF), going head-to-head with the F-16 in that competition. Clearly, the F-20 was no longer campaigned as a limited fighter; it was state-of-the-art for the mission. By this time, Northrop had invested more than $1 billion in the privately funded Tigershark. If the F-20 could garner the U.S. Air Force contract, it might be worth $4 billion, as well as opening the door to foreign sales that were slow to materialize.[150]

With a company F-5F chase plane escorting it, the F-5G first tested its wings at Edwards Air Force Base on 30 August 1982. (AFFTC/HO collection)

During initial weapons launching demonstrations over the Navy's China Lake ranges in the last half of 1983, a Northrop F-20 released an air-to-air missile from its left wingtip rail. Ford Aerospace made the AIM-9 Sidewinder missile launched in the photo. (AFFTC/HO collection)

The second F-20 was photographed during assembly at Northrop's Production Development Center in Hawthorne, California. (Northrop via AFFTC/HO collection)

Northrop's specialized turning jigs allowed workers, circa 1983, to access the F-20 forward fuselage from many angles at reasonable working heights. (Northrop via AFFTC/HO collection)

The F-20 could carry a "buddy" system refueling store to enable it to refuel other aircraft. Many photos of F-20s show civil registration numbers assigned, such as N4416T, to these company-produced aircraft. (AFFTC/HO collection)

Later that year, the Air Force decided to modify 270 existing F-16s instead of buying either new F-16s or the F-20 for the ADF role. The competition had been rough at times. If Northrop proponents touted the F-20 as less expensive to buy and maintain, F-16 supporters pointed out the fact that the F-16 already in the Air Force inventory meant its logistics pipeline was already in place. When the dust settled, only four F-20s were ever ordered, a commitment by Bahrain who already flew F-5Es. Some potential foreign customers indicated they might buy F-20s if the U.S. military did as well. With no other Tigersharks to be built, Northrop stopped work on the number four airframe and closed the project in

Two gray F-20s in flight show canopy differences; distant aircraft (N3986B) has more extensive glazing intended to give the pilot more rearward visibility. (AFFTC/HO collection)

December 1986. The Bahrainian order, which would have been too costly to complete because of its small size, went unfilled.

Pundits said Northrop's private billion-dollar venture with the F-20 would likely not be repeated any time soon in the U.S. aerospace industry since it ended with no production. Other observers, inside and outside the company, noted that the F-20 had propelled Northrop from its comfortable role as a supplier of modest export fighters to a position as a cutting-edge design and development team; a team that understood the new and evolving world of sophisticated aircraft systems.

The sole surviving F-20 is displayed in Los Angeles' California Science Center.

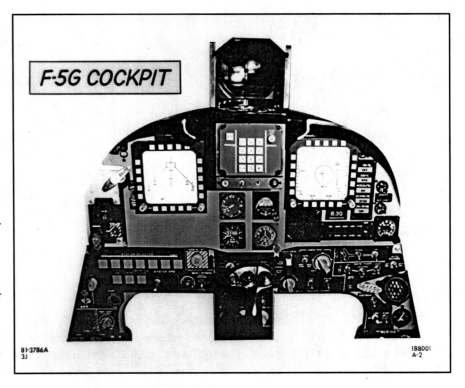

Above: Early depiction of F-5G cockpit layout shows drag chute handle to left of left-hand flat panel screen display. Below the lower right corner of that same screen is an all-stores jettison button surrounded by tiger stripe warning markings. (AFFTC/HO collection)

Above: During their relatively short test and demonstration careers, the three F-20As went through many paint variations including a large inward-slanting F-20 tail marking on aircraft number 82-0062. Lower fuselage ledge, which maintained desirable flight characteristics similar to those of the F-5E, is visible between the wing trailing edge and horizontal stabilizer. (AFFTC/HO collection)

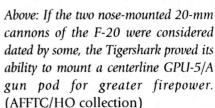

Left: Tigershark N4416T (82-0062) releases a stick of five streamlined bombs over a California test range. Wingtip AIM-9 missiles indicate an ability for the F-20 to protect itself from aerial threats even while carrying out ground attack missions. (AFFTC/HO collection)

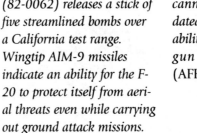

Above: If the two nose-mounted 20-mm cannons of the F-20 were considered dated by some, the Tigershark proved its ability to mount a centerline GPU-5/A gun pod for greater firepower. (AFFTC/HO collection)

APPENDIX 1

Specifications

	Length	Span	Height	Max Wt.	Top Speed	Cruise	Engine	Max Thrust
F-5A	47'2"	25'10"	13'6"	20,040 lbs	925 mph	575 mph	2xJ85-GE-13	4,080 lbs ea.
F-5B		25'10"	13'1"				2xJ85-GE-13	4,080 lbs ea.
CF-5A	47'2"	25'10"	13'6"				2xJ85-GE-15	4,300 lbs ea.
F-5E	48'2" 47'5"*	26'8"	13'4"	25,350 lbs	Mach 1.63	650 mph	2xJ85-GE-21	5,000 lbs ea.
F-5F	51'8" 50'11"*	26'8"	13'2"	22,028 lbs	Mach 1.57		2xJ85-GE-21	5,000 lbs ea.
F-20	46'7"	26'8"	13'10"	27,500 lbs	Mach 2		1xF404	18,000 lbs
T-38A	46'4.5"	25'3"	12'10"	12,050 lbs	820 mph		2xJ85-GE-5	3,850 lbs ea.

*Sharknose variation

(The compilation of aircraft specifications can be surprisingly inexact, with some tables rounding fractions and decimalizing them. With the caveat that some of these numbers vary slightly from source to source, this table provides a quick overview of F-5 evolution.)

Significant Dates

October 1956 - USAF approved Northrop's TZ-156 design, later to become the T-38.

May 1958 - USAF, on behalf of Department of Defense, issued letter of intent authorizing Northrop to build three prototype N-156F fighters.

10 April 1959 - T-38 first flight, at Edwards AFB by Lew Nelson.

30 July 1959 - N-156F first flight (aircraft 59-4987), at Edwards AFB by Lew Nelson.

February 1961 - T-38 flight test program completed with 2,000 flights.

May 1962 - Department of Defense announced selection of N-156F for use in foreign Military Assistance Program (MAP).

31 July 1963 - First flight of YF-5A (the third N-156F refurbished), at Edwards AFB by Hank Chouteau.

February 1964 - First flight of prototype F-5B two-seater, at Edwards AFB.

20–23 October 1965 - USAF Skoshi Tiger F-5C aircraft deploy by air from Williams AFB, Arizona, to South Vietnam.

5 December 1965 - Skoshi Tiger squadron logs its 1,000[th] combat sortie in Vietnam, flown by Col. Frank N. Emory, commander of the Skoshi Tiger task force.

7 December 1965 - Skoshi Tiger F-5 64-13318, flown by Maj. Joseph B. Baggett, becomes first F-5A to complete 100 combat missions.

16 December 1965 - Only F-5 loss during Skoshi Tiger combat evaluation; enemy ground fire responsible. Pilot Maj. Joseph B. Baggett rescued, but subsequently died due to injuries received.

28 February 1966 - Skoshi Tiger F-5s bombed targets in North Vietnam for the first time.

28 March 1969 - First flight of testbed YF-5B-21 (sometimes referred to simply as F-5-21), at Edwards AFB by General Electric test pilot John Fritz.

8 December 1970 - Northrop received a fixed-price incentive contract for engineering development and production of the new model F-5-21 (later F-5E).

23 June 1972 - Rollout of the F-5E.

31 January 1972 - Final T-38 delivered to USAF at Palmdale, California.

11 August 1972 - F-5E first flight, by Northrop test pilot Hank Chouteau. F-5E 71-1417 had been trucked to Edwards AFB on 10 July in preparation for its first flight.

14 August 1974 - Rollout of the F-5F.

25 September 1974 - F-5F first flight.

30 August 1982 - F-5G (later F-20) first flight, by Northrop pilot Russ Scott, one month ahead of schedule.

From the Laboratory: Radical Experiments

The F-5's availability and its long-nosed geometry suited testers in search of airframes that could be customized radically to prove advanced aerodynamic concepts.

X-29

Advancements in fly-by-wire computer-driven flight controls enabled the unstable shape of the forward-swept wing X-29 to be flown safely by a research pilot. The coincidental development of composite materials strong and light enough to survive the unique stresses imposed on a forward-swept wing made construction possible. Some economy in the creation of the two testbed X-29s was achieved by using portions of F-5A fuselages. The resulting research aircraft, powered by a single GE F404 turbofan, was built by Grumman years before the merger of Northrop with Grumman.

First flown in 1984, the two X-29s were the stars of a prolific flight test program that lasted into 1992, and demonstrated maneuvering and handling qualities improvements at high angles of attack. Airflow over a forward-swept wing migrates inboard so that at high angles of attack, the outboard control surfaces remain effective, promoting the X-29's maneuverability at high angles of attack where traditional wings could lose effectiveness in an aerodynamic stall. In 1985 one X-29 became the first forward-swept wing aircraft to exceed Mach 1 in level flight. The body of research created by the X-29 program involves a number of aeronautical disciplines.

The ability of forward-swept wings to cope with maneuverability

This look-down view of the X-29 research aircraft in flight over California's Mojave Desert shows its striking and unique forward swept wing and canard design. (NASA)

issues had long been suspected; Germany worked on such designs during World War II, and North American Aviation created a paper proposal for a derivative of the famed P-51 Mustang that called for a forward-swept wing. But traditional airframe structures of the 1940s were inadequate to cope with the loads imposed on such a design.[15]

At the end of the X-29 program, one of the experimental jets was placed on display at the NASA Dryden Flight Research Center on Edwards Air Force Base in California; the other was sent to the National Museum of the United States Air Force at Wright-Patterson Air Force Base, Ohio.

F-5 Shaped Sonic Boom Demonstration

In August 2003, a radically altered F-5E with a deepened and resculpted forward fuselage demonstrated sonic boom levels measurably lower than those for an unmodified F-5E. Northrop described the tests: "The Shaped Sonic Boom Demonstration (SSBD) team conducted back-to-back supersonic flights of an F-5E with a modified airframe and an unmodified F-5E at NASA's Dryden Flight Research Center at Edwards Air Force Base, California. Comparison of the sound pressure waves created by the two aircraft showed a significant reduction in sonic boom intensity for the modified aircraft.

Results of the demonstration could lead eventually to the production of new aircraft with noticeably quieter sonic booms."[152]

The tests involved a Navy Top Gun F-5E from NAS Fallon, Nevada, as the baseline aircraft. The sonic boom measurements for the modified F-5E showed improvements, but as of this writing the technology needs more development before it can yield supersonic aircraft with sonic boom signatures low enough to be acceptable for flight over populated areas. If this can be achieved, it promises to accelerate commercial aircraft speeds by overcoming a hurdle that required the SST to limit its supersonic speeds to tracks over unpopulated regions like oceans.

Although the incredible aesthetics of the F-5 series were lost with this shaped sonic boom demonstrator nose and forward fuselage modification of an E-model, the resulting test flights encouraged engineers that the shape of future supersonic aircraft might lessen the severity of sonic booms. (Photo by Tony Chong—Skyshadow Studios)

ENDNOTES

1. Richard Sweeney, "Fang Stayed in Mockup Stage, But Paid Test Bed Dividends," Aviation Week, June 4, 1956, Pp. 38-39.

2. "Northrop F-5E case study in aircraft design," William G. Stuart, 1978, (item UGH 3227.F5 N6 in the U.S. Air Force Academy Cadet Library).

3. Ibid.

4. Fred Anderson, Northrop – An Aeronautical History, published by Northrop Corp., Los Angeles, 1976.

5. "Northrop F-5E case study in aircraft design," William G. Stuart, 1978, (item UGH 3227.F5 N6 in the U.S. Air Force Academy Cadet Library).

6. F-5A Project Data, prepared by F-5A Tool Project Engineering, September 1962, revised October 1964.

7. Ibid.

8. Ibid.

9. "Northrop F-5E case study in aircraft design," William G. Stuart, 1978, (item UGH 3227.F5 N6 in the U.S. Air Force Academy Cadet Library).

10. F-5A Project Data, prepared by F-5A Tool Project Engineering, September 1962, revised October 1964.

11. Ibid.

12. Ibid.

13. Ibid.

14. Gordon Swanborough and Peter M. Bowers, United States Military Aircraft Since 1908, Putnam, London, 1971.

15. F-5A Project Data, prepared by F-5A Tool Project Engineering, September 1962, revised October 1964.

16. Ibid.

17. Document, "Test Item Description," (T-38A aircraft modified to T-38C configuration), AFFTC History Office files, undated.

18. Gordon Swanborough and Peter M. Bowers, United States Military Aircraft Since 1908, Putnam, London, 1971.

19. "Northrop F-5E case study in aircraft design," William G. Stuart, 1978, (item UGH 3227.F5 N6 in the U.S. Air Force Academy Cadet Library).

20. Gordon Swanborough and Peter M. Bowers, United States Military Aircraft Since 1908, Putnam, London, 1971.

21. "Louver Doors Increase Engine Air on F-5A," Aviation Week & Space Technology, June 28, 1965, P. 52.

22. Fred Anderson, Northrop – An Aeronautical History, published by Northrop Corp., Los Angeles, 1976.

23. Fact Sheet, "F-5 Tactical Fighter Modernization," Northrop Grumman Integrated Systems, undated, available on Web December 2005.

24. Ibid.

25. John W. R. Taylor, editor, Combat Aircraft of the World, Putnam, New York, 1969 and 1979.

26. Website www.scramble.nl, Dutch Aviation Society/Scramble.

27. Ibid.

28. Ibid.

29. Ibid.

30. Joe Baugher, Website www.fitertown.com.

31. Edward H. Kolcum, "Arab Pilots to Train at Wheelus," Aviation Week & Space Technology, March 23, 1970, Pp. 14-16.

32. Joe Baugher, Website www.fitertown.com.

33. Ibid.

34. "Dutch Order 105 F-5 Aircraft," Aviation Week & Space Technology, Feb. 6, 1967, P. 36.

35. F-5A Project Data, prepared by F-5A Tool Project Engineering, Sep-tember 1962, revised October 1964.

36. "Arabians Study F-5," Aviation Week & Space Technology, Aug. 3, 1964, P. 21.

37. See also Joe Baugher, Web site www.fitertown.com, and Web site www.scramble.nl, Dutch Aviation Society/Scramble.

38. Republic of Korea Air Force Web site www.airforce.mil.kr

39. "Northrop F-5E case study in aircraft design," William G. Stuart, 1978, (item UGH 3227.F5 N6 in the U.S. Air Force Academy Cadet Library).

40. C.M. Plattner, "The War in Vietnam: Force Buildup Keyed to Wider Escalation," Aviation Week & Space Technology, Jan. 3, 1966, Pp. 16-21.

41. "F-5 Buy Planned to Bolster USAF, VNAF," Aviation Week & Space Technology, Aug. 1, 1966, Pp. 19-20.

42. Joe Baugher, Web site www.fitertown.com.

43. Ibid.

44. Data compiled and furnished by Barrett Tillman.

45. James P. Coyne, Airpower in the Gulf, Air Force Association/Aero-space Education Foundation, Arling-ton, Va., 1992.

46. Logistics Support to Southeast Asia by San Antonio Air Materiel Area (U), Calendar Year 1966, Vol. 1, Historical Monograph No. 16, Hq SAAMA, Kelly AFB, Texas (declassi-fied 3 Apr 87).

47. History of Skoshi Tiger (U), (4503rd Tactical Fighter Squadron, Provisional), 23 July 1965 – 10 March 1966, by John C. Brassell, USAF TAWC Historian.

48. Final Report – Combat Evalu-ation of the F-5 Aircraft – "Skoshi Tiger" (U), Tactical Air Command, USAF Tactical Air Warfare Center,

Eglin Air Force Base, Florida, April 1966 (declassified Aug 97).

49. Interview, author with Challen "Choni" Irvine, 16 Dec 2005.

50. Final Report – Combat Evaluation of the F-5 Aircraft – "Skoshi Tiger" (U), Tactical Air Command, USAF Tactical Air Warfare Center, Eglin Air Force Base, Florida, April 1966 (declassified Aug 97).

51. Ibid.

52. Ibid.

53. Ibid.

54. Ibid.

55. Ibid.

56. History of Skoshi Tiger (U), (4503rd Tactical Fighter Squadron, Provisional), 23 July 1965 – 10 March 1966, by John C. Brassell, USAF TAWC Historian.

57. Ibid.

58. Ibid.

59. Ibid.

60. History of Pacific Air Forces Base Command (6486th Air Base Wing), 1 July 1965 – 31 December 1965, Vol. 2, by Historical Division, Office of Information, Pacific Air Forces Base Command, Jean A. Sproule, Historian.

61. Final Report – Combat Evaluation of the F-5 Aircraft – "Skoshi Tiger" (U), Tactical Air Command, USAF Tactical Air Warfare Center, Eglin Air Force Base, Florida, April 1966 (declassified Aug 97).

62. History of Skoshi Tiger (U), (4503rd Tactical Fighter Squadron, Provisional), 23 July 1965 – 10 March 1966, by John C. Brassell, USAF TAWC Historian.

63. Ibid.

64. History of Skoshi Tiger (U), (4503rd Tactical Fighter Squadron, Provisional), 23 July 1965 – 10 March 1966, by John C. Brassell, USAF TAWC Historian, and Final Report – Combat Evaluation of the F-5 Aircraft – "Skoshi Tiger" (U), Tactical Air Command, USAF Tactical Air

Warfare Center, Eglin Air Force Base, Florida, April 1966 (declassified Aug 97).

65. History of Skoshi Tiger (U), (4503rd Tactical Fighter Squadron, Provisional), 23 July 1965 – 10 March 1966, by John C. Brassell, USAF TAWC Historian.

66. Ibid.

67. Ibid.

68. Ibid.

69. Ibid.

70. Final Report – Combat Evaluation of the F-5 Aircraft – "Skoshi Tiger" (U), Tactical Air Command, USAF Tactical Air Warfare Center, Eglin Air Force Base, Florida, April 1966 (declassified Aug 97).

71. Data extracted by the Air Force Skoshi Tiger historian from the Skoshi Tiger F-5 Combat Evaluation Operations Report.

72. Logistics Support to Southeast Asia by San Antonio Air Materiel Area (U), Calendar Year 1966, Vol. 1, Historical Monograph No. 16, Hq SAAMA, Kelly AFB, Texas (declassified 3 Apr 87).

73. Interview, author with Bob Titus, 16 December 2005.

74. History of Skoshi Tiger (U), (4503rd Tactical Fighter Squadron, Provisional), 23 July 1965 – 10 March 1966, by John C. Brassell, USAF TAWC Historian.

75. Ibid.

76. Ibid.

77. Ibid.

78. Final Report – Combat Evaluation of the F-5 Aircraft – "Skoshi Tiger" (U), Tactical Air Command, USAF Tactical Air Warfare Center, Eglin Air Force Base, Florida, April 1966 (declassified Aug 97).

79. Ibid.

80. Ibid.

81. Ibid.

82. Ibid.

83. Ibid.

84. Ibid.

85. Ibid.

86. Ibid.

87. Ibid.

88. Ibid.

89. Ibid.

90. Ibid.

91. Ibid.

92. Ibid.

93. Ibid.

94. Ibid.

95. Ibid.

96. E-mail, Bob Titus to author, Subject: F-5, 31 Oct 05.

97. Final Report – Combat Evaluation of the F-5 Aircraft – "Skoshi Tiger" (U), Tactical Air Command, USAF Tactical Air Warfare Center, Eglin Air Force Base, Florida, April 1966 (declassified Aug 97).

98. E-mail, John Lisella to Bob Titus, Subject: F-5, 31 Oct 05.

99. E-mail, Bob Titus to author, Subject: F-5, 31 Oct 05.

100 E-mail, Bob Titus to author, Subject: F-5, 30 Oct 05.

101. Ibid.

102. E-mail, Bill Rippy to Bob Titus, 31 Oct 05.

103. Fred Anderson, Northrop – An Aeronautical History, published by Northrop Corp., Los Angeles, 1976.

104. Ibid.

105. Gordon Swanborough and Peter M. Bowers, United States Military Aircraft Since 1908, Putnam, London, 1971.

106. Fred Anderson, Northrop – An Aeronautical History, published by Northrop Corp., Los Angeles, 1976.

107. Fact Sheet, "T-38 Talon," U.S. Air Force.

108. Fact Sheet, "T-38 Supersonic Trainer," Integrated Systems, Northrop Grumman Corp., 01/02.

109. David M. North, "NASA's Hot Rod," Aviation Week & Space Technology, May 3, 2004, Pp. 64-65.

110. Ibid.

111. T-38 rated Mach number is sometimes listed as 1.25; consistency

in performance measurements remains elusive, with variables affecting measured outcomes.

112. Ibid.

113. "GE Tests Advanced J85 Turbojet Engine," Aviation Week & Space Technology, Aug. 18, 1969, P. 58.

114. "F-5 Genealogy," F-5 Technical Digest, Northrop, Feb. 1979, Pp. 8-9.

115. U.S. General Accounting Office Staff Study, "F-5E International Fighter Aircraft," Department of the Air Force, February 1973.

116. "F-5 Genealogy," F-5 Technical Digest, Northrop, Feb. 1979, Pp. 8-9.

117. From notes to this manuscript provided by Northrop F-5 engineer Ron Gibb.

118. USAF Series F-5E/F Flight Manual, T.O. 1F-5E-1, 1 August 1984, Change 9 – 15 November 1990.

119. Letter, "F-5E Joint Test Force Quarterly Historical Report," by Lt. Col. Joseph P. Waters, Director, F-5E Joint Test Force, 12 Oct 72, and letter, "F-5E Joint Test Force Quarterly Historical Report (Oct-Dec 72)," by Maj. John H. Taylor, Director, F-5E Joint Test Force, 19 Jan 73.

120. Letter, "F-5E Joint Test Force Quarterly Historical Report (Jan-Mar 73)," by Maj. John H. Taylor, Director, F-5E Joint Test Force, 19 Apr 73.

121. Ibid.

122. Letter, "F-5E Joint Test Force Quarterly Historical Report (Apr-Jun 73)," by Maj. John H. Taylor, Director, F-5E Joint Test Force, undated.

123. Letter, "F-5E/F Joint Test Force Historical Report for July through December 1974," by Lt. Col. John H. Taylor, Director, F-5E Joint Test Force, 24 Jan 75.

124. Ibid.

125. Memo For Record, "F-5E Spin Susceptibility Test Safety Review," 7 Jan 1976, attached to "F-5E/F JTF History, July thru September 1975," by Capt. John E. Savage, F-5F Maintenance Officer, 8 October 1975.

126. Letter, "F-5E/F JTF History, January thru March 1976," by MSgt. Joseph K. Dahl, NCOIC, AFTEC F-5 Test Force, 6 April 1976. (History of the TAC element of the F-5E/F JTF.)

127. Letter, "F-5 Joint Test Force Historical Report for January through June 1976," by Maj. J.H. Manly, Director, F-5 JTF, 29 June 1976.

128. Letter, "F-5 Joint Test Force Historical Report for July through December 1976," by Maj. R.J. Hegstrom, Deputy Director, F-5 JTF, 5 January 1977.

129. Letter, "F-5E/F Joint Test Force Historical Report for July through December 1974," by Lt. Col. John H. Taylor, Director, F-5E Joint Test Force, 24 Jan 75.

130. Letter, "F-5 Joint Test Force Historical Report for January through June 1976," by Maj. J.H. Manly, Director, F-5 JTF, 29 June 1976.

131. Letter, "F-5 Joint Test Force Historical Report for July through December 1976," by Maj. R.J. Hegstrom, Deputy Director, F-5 JTF, 5 January 1977.

132. Ibid.

133. Letter, "F-5 Joint Test Force Historical Report for January through June 1977," by Lt. Col. J.H. Manly, Director, F-5 JTF, 14 July 1977.

134. Letter, "F-5E/F JTF History, July through September 1977," by Capt. Marty J. Cavato, F-5 AFTEC/IOT&E Deputy Test Director, 29 Sep 1977. (History of the TAC element of the F-5E/F JTF.)

135. Statement of Capability (Unclassified), RF-5E Development Test and Evaluation, Air Force Flight Test Center, 14 Dec 82, revised 15 Mar 83.

136. Ibid.

137. Ibid.

138. "RF-5E Reconnaissance Aircraft – New Tiger Sees and Tells All," F-5 Technical Digest, Northrop, Feb. 1979, Pp. 10-11.

139. Ibid.

140. Ibid.

141. Interview, author with Ron Gibb, December 2005.

142. "RF-5E Reconnaissance Aircraft – New Tiger Sees and Tells All," F-5 Technical Digest, Northrop, Feb. 1979, Pp. 10-11.

143. Statement of Capability (Unclassified), RF-5E Development Test and Evaluation, Air Force Flight Test Center, 14 Dec 82, revised 15 Mar 83.

144. Joe Baugher, Web site www.fitertown.com.

145. "Northrop F-5G Makes Its First Flight," Aviation Week & Space Technology, September 6, 1982.

146. "F-20 Tigershark Tactical Fighter," Northrop Corp. Public Relations news release, 4/28/83.

147. "The Airplane Nobody Wanted," by Ralph Wetterhahn, Air & Space, August/September 2000, Pp. 86-95.

148. "No. 4 F-20 Configured With Production Changes," Aviation Week & Space Technology, February 25, 1985, Pp. 55-56.

149. Ibid.

150. "F-20 – Northrop Jet in Shoot-Out With Dynamics' F-16," by Ralph Vartabedian, reprint from Los Angeles Times, May 11, 1986.

151. Frederick A. Johnsen, North American P-51 Mustang, WarbirdTech Series Vol. 5, Specialty Press, North Branch, Minnesota, 1996.

152. News Release, "Northrop Grumman Engineers Honored With Aircraft Design Award from American Institute of Aeronautics and Astronautics," Sept. 22, 2004.

CPSIA information can be obtained at www.ICGtesting.com
Printed in the USA
LVOW09s0042091013

356079LV00008B/105/P